IDEOLOGY IN CONFLICT

Communist Political Theory

Edited and with an Introductory Essay by

DIETER DUX

Professor of Political Science
University of Cincinnati

W99

D. VAN NOSTRAND COMPANY, INC.

PRINCETON, NEW JERSEY

TORONTO   LONDON

NEW YORK

D. VAN NOSTRAND COMPANY, INC.
120 Alexander St., Princeton, New Jersey
(*Principal Office*)
24 West 40 Street, New York 18, New York

D. VAN NOSTRAND COMPANY, LTD.
358, Kensington High Street, London, W.14, England

D. VAN NOSTRAND COMPANY (Canada), LTD.
25 Hollinger Road, Toronto 16, Canada

Preface

For some years now even the casual reader of American news media has been made aware of the increasing difficulties encountered by the members of the Socialist camp in preserving a meaningful degree of unity. Theoretical arguments about the definition of peaceful coexistence, the inevitability and consequences of war, the nature of the transition from a capitalistic society to Socialism, the content and scope of proletarian internationalism, have produced not only acrimonious debates, political and economic sanctions, but the exclusion—voluntary or involuntary—of two Communist-led states from the Socialist bloc.

This volume was prepared to shed some light, through the use of primary documents, on this controversy for the period from the 20th Congress of the C.P.S.U. in February, 1956, to the 22nd Congress in October, 1961. Within this time span of nearly six years, experimentation with formulae designed to preserve the desired degree of bloc unity included at one extreme the encouragement of a considerable degree of national diversity and at the other the application of military force to prevent disunity.

The project was originally undertaken at the suggestion of Professor H. M. Vinacke and resulted in a paper prepared for a Conference on United States Foreign Policy, sponsored jointly by the Johnson Foundation and the Department of Political Science at the University of Cincinnati in December, 1960.

I am indebted to Mrs. C. C. Thomas for typing the manuscript and to my wife Marilyn for providing editorial assistance and the requisite degree of domestic tranquillity.

DIETER DUX

Cincinnati, Ohio
March, 1963

Table of Contents

INTRODUCTION

I

The basic assumption on which this introduction rests is that the recent tensions between the Soviet Union, Yugoslavia, and China can best be understood in terms of the evolution of Communism from a single-country base to a polycentered system.

Consequently, it will be argued that the emergence of Belgrade and Peking as political centers with separate and sometimes divisive national interests could not but disturb the monolithic unity of the Communist world.

Nearly all the language of this dispute has suggested that the issues between the Soviet Union and its lesser associates concerned questions of ideological differences, implying that non-ideological issues could safely be by-passed. This approach finds support and encouragement in the well known tendency of Communism to depend upon the Marxist-Leninist system to evaluate events, actions, and attitudes.

Lenin is the source of countless familiar quotations stressing the overwhelming importance of ideological unity based on Marxist theory as the precondition for the success of the Socialist movement. Stalin, Khrushchev, Mao, Tito—indeed, all the important members of the Communist elite—can be cited on the same point with equal facility. Moreover, it is not only the success of the revolutionary movement that is dependent on Marxist revolutionary theory; the personal fortunes and careers of the leading members of the elite are also deeply influenced by considerations of ideology.

Molotov had to apologize for having incorrectly evaluated the Socialist stage achieved in the Soviet Union in 1955. ". . . I consider my formula . . . from which the conclusion can be drawn that only the foundations of a Socialist society have been built in the Soviet Union, as theoretically mistaken. . . ." [1]

Marshall Zhukov was demoted in 1957 for having "violated the Leninist principles of guiding the armed

1

forces. . . ." [2] The anti-party group of Malenkov, Kaganovich and Molotov were expelled from the party because ". . . they are sectarian and dogmatic and they use a scholastic inert approach to Marxism-Leninism." [3]

When Mao resigned the chairmanship of the Communist Chinese government in 1958, one explanation among several given for this step was that he would ". . . also be enabled to set aside more time for Marxist-Leninist theoretical work." [4]

Given the preferred position assigned to Marxist theory within Communist Societies, it is somewhat surprising to learn that Dialectical Materialism—which "reflects the Universal Law of the development of nature, society and human thought" and which "is valid for the past, the present, and the future"—is said, by reliable sources, to be subject to creative modification.[5]

Stalin, quoting Lenin, said that ". . . 'revolutionary theory is not a dogma,' that it 'undergoes final formulation only when brought in close contact with practice in the actual . . . revolutionary movement . . .' for it ought to be verified by the data obtained from practice." [6]

The Yugoslavian League of Communists Program of 1958 was less obtuse in subordinating theory to practice: ". . . Marxists cannot permit any form or means of struggle to become a principle or dogma preventing the application, at a given time and place, of such forms of political action, as would answer the conditions of the struggle, life, and concepts of the working class, and the progressive social forces in general."

The December 1957 issue of "News Front" attributed the following statement to Mao Tse-tung: "We must carefully select and use materials on the basis of objective facts, and, under the guidance of the general laws of Marxism-Leninism reach a correct conclusion after an analysis of these materials. Such a conclusion is a scientific conclusion, not an empty conclusion. Such an attitude is meant to derive the truth from the facts. . . ."

II

During the lifetime of Stalin, "creative Marxism" did not encounter any particular difficulties, since the evolution of doctrine emanated from a single source. Like all monistic systems, Marxism-Leninism's tendency toward rigidity set limits to ideological reinterpretation, but so long as circumstances seemed to require it Stalin approached the problem of modification with a good deal of flexibility. Heretical tendencies or deviations were incorporated or discouraged. Sometimes the reformulation of ideology anticipated a desired condition: peaceful coexistence with Capitalism came to be described as the definitive relationship of Capitalism and Socialism during the middle 1920's; at other times ideology was "enriched" to justify political realities *ex post facto,* as was the case in Stalin's "single-country Socialism" theory.

It is, of course, not implied that Stalin's creative interpretation of Marxism-Leninism stripped the original theory of Communism of all content. It is too obvious to merit extensive comment that all modern-day Marxists believe as firmly as their intellectual antecedents in the ultimate victory of Socialism over competing ideologies. The disagreements within the Socialist camp as to whether this happy event will require a Socialist burying party or will result from resigned Capitalist self-immolation is an argument about means and strategy.

Among the basic elements of Marxism that have survived the Stalinist regime relatively unchanged, two are of primary importance: the concept of Dictatorship of the Proletariat, and the Class Struggle.

The retention of the first concept within the ideological framework of Soviet theory was essential to maintain and justify in theoretical terms the dominant position of the Communist party in Soviet society after 1917. It will be recalled that the original definition of the Dictatorship of the Proletariat as developed by Marx had read as follows: "The Proletariat organized as the ruling class." Lenin in 1917, prior to the Revolution, suggested a more suitable definition: "the organization of the advance-guard of the oppressed as the ruling class." The Constitution of 1936 further developed the manipulative possibilities of the Communist party by assigning it the responsibility of "the leading core of all organizations of the working people, Public and Private." It remained only for the Party to add to its rules the principle of democratic centralism to insure unity of policy as well as ideology.

Similarly, the concept of the class struggle proved a

device useful to the operation of a totalitarian system. Applied in a variety of ways, it gave the semblance of reason to the maintenance of state machinery after the revolution, sustained the revolutionary fervor of the population, and helped identify the enemy.

Under Stalin's rule other constituent parts of Marxism, such as the nature of subsequent proletarian revolutions in Capitalist countries and the timing of the transition from Socialism to Communism in the Soviet Union were treated with rigidity or flexibility as the exigencies of Soviet internal or foreign relations seemed to require. The certainty that all erosions of doctrine could be brought short by the application of democratic centralism made ideological flexibility something less than dangerous.

Not only did these rules serve to maintain unity within the Russian Communist Party, but their observance by non-Russian Communists was assured at an early date by the adoption of a resolution at the 1920 Congress of the Communist International.

Consequently, during the Stalinist period a single center guided the whole Communist camp, giving primary attention to the building of Socialism in a single country and guiding the non-Russian Communist parties (through the instrument of the Comintern) in the pursuit of policies devoted to the same overriding goal. The emergence of independent centers of Communism after World War II—such as Yugoslavia and, later, China—produced profound changes in the relations of Moscow to the newly established peripheral Communist states. The significance of these changes entirely escaped Stalin. His world view, unchanged since the victory over Trotsky, continued to include an essentially pessimistic attitude about the chances of Communism to expand beyond the heartland. The overwhelming strength of the Capitalist states and their allies would require unflinching devotion on the part of Communists everywhere to the effort of reconstructing the central economic base destroyed by the war. Such expansion of the Communist system as did occur after 1945 was required to further protect the weak "Socialist island" surrounded by a "rough Capitalist sea."

The integration of these dependent satellites into the Soviet imperial system proved not particularly difficult during Stalin's day. The ease with which Stalin had managed the non-Russian Communist parties prior to 1945 made it seem reasonable to apply to the Eastern European satellites the techniques of control that had proved effective before. While Stalin's judgment about his ability to maneuver the satellites into a position of total dependence on the Soviet Union proved entirely correct, his attitude toward Yugoslavia and China helped lay the ground work for their current quarrel.

The long list of mistaken policies can be reduced to two. In the first place, it seemed inconceivable to Stalin that indigenous Communist parties could seize power in either Yugoslavia or China without the active intervention of the Soviet army. Tito was told during the war, when he unfolded his plan for the Communist seizure of the Yugoslavian state machinery, that the time was not ripe for this, since the bourgeoisie was too strong. The best advice that Tito received from Stalin was to fight for Communist party representation in a coalition government under a monarchy. Stalin's assessment of the revolutionary possibilities in China was no more correct. In 1948 he admitted to the Yugoslav Kardelj: "We have also made mistakes. For instance, after the war we invited the Chinese comrades to come to Moscow and we discussed the situation in China. We told them bluntly that we considered the development of the uprising in China had no prospect, and that the Chinese comrades should seek a *modus vivendi* with Chiang, that they should join the China government and dissolve their army." [7]

In the second place, Stalin demonstrated complete inability to comprehend the emergence of national Communism in Yugoslavia as a way of life requiring new adjustments of the internal relations of the camp of Socialism. The evidence is presented by Khrushchev in his "secret" report to the 20th Congress of the C.P.S.U.

". . . I was invited to visit Stalin who, pointing to the copy of a letter lately sent to Tito, asked me, 'Have you read this?'

"Not waiting for my reply he answered, 'I will shake my little finger—and there will be no more Tito. He will fall.'

"We have paid dearly for this, shaking of the little finger. Tito did not fall. Why? The reason was, that, in this case of disagreement with the Yugoslav comrades, Tito had behind him a state and a people who had gone through a severe school of fighting for liberty and independence, a people which gave support to its leaders."

The roots of the Yugoslav-Soviet dispute reach back at least to the last years of World War II. Though generally considered a trusted ally by the Soviet Union, Tito and his associates on many occasions complained about the lack of Soviet material assistance and at the same time resisted any large-scale introduction of Soviet military elements into Yugoslav home territory. This general intransigence of Yugoslavia and its stubborn insistence that the job of liberating Yugoslavia be done "Yugoslavia's way" proved irritating but manageable from the Soviet point of view.

A speech by Marshal Tito in May 1945 destroyed whatever confidence the Soviet Union may have had about its ability to manipulate the Yugoslavians into a position of dependence on the Soviet Union. Tito stated on that occasion in Ljubljana: "It is said that this is a just war and we have considered it as such. However, we seek also a just end; we demand that everyone shall be master in his own house; we do not want to pay for others; we do not want to be used as a bribe in international bargaining; we do not want to get involved in any policy of spheres of interest. . . ."

The Russian ambassador promptly criticized the speech, indicating that his country could not tolerate any further unfriendly gestures from the Yugoslav Peoples Front which, it was charged, did not take instructions in the Leninist tradition.

It is possible and convenient to divide the post-war history of Yugoslav-Soviet relations into two distinct time periods. Both periods ended in the severance of mutual ties: in 1948 Yugoslavia was expelled from the Cominform; in 1958 the accusation of Revisionism separated it no less completely from the Soviet camp.

Both crises were preceded by a period during which the Soviet Union attempted to tighten the lines of control throughout the Socialist world in response to developments viewed as threatening the Soviet national interest. In essence, then, the ultimate cause of conflict may be said to have arisen from the inability of two sovereign states—sharing a common ideology—to adjust their relations within a security community in a manner satisfactory to both parties. For the Soviet Union the issue became the preservation of "the leading role" of the "largest Socialist state"; for Yugoslavia it always remained a question of ensuring "equality between the big and the small, between the strong and the weak, between the developed and the underdeveloped. Only this is Socialist equality of peoples and states." [8]

During the period preceding the crisis of 1948, relations between the Soviet Union and Yugoslavia deteriorated progressively. The conduct of the Red Army on Yugoslav territory was not that of an ally on friendly soil. Mistreatment of civilians was common. Of more serious consequence was the obvious attempt of Soviet officers to infiltrate and dominate the Yugoslav army. The disposition of the Trieste problem placed additional strains on the relations between the two countries. While Molotov had initially sponsored the Yugoslav position at the 1946 Foreign Ministers Conference, he soon abandoned it and accepted the compromise formula worked out by France. The Yugoslavian government had no prior information of this unilateral shift in joint policy and interpreted it as an indication of Soviet willingness to sacrifice Yugoslav interests for the sake of improved relations with the Italian Communists. The deliberate frustrations by the Soviet Union of other Yugoslav territorial aspirations in the Balkan area led to increasing irritation. But above all, the Soviet sponsored device of the joint stock company became symptomatic of the Soviet attitude toward the "weak" and "underdeveloped" associates in the Socialist Commonwealth. In August 1946, negotiations began between the two countries to develop a series of joint stock companies which, it was the hope of Yugoslavia, would help develop an indigenous industrial base. According to Dedijer, the Yugoslavs soon discovered that the Soviets had little interest in promoting their country's industrialization. "What do you need heavy industry for," asked the Russian representative, "in the Urals we have everything you need." Under those circumstances Yugoslavia rejected the proposals.

However, in February 1947 a new start was made. Two companies were created: "Justa" for air transport and "Juspad" for river transportation.

The obvious Yugoslavian disillusionment with the operation of these two joint stock companies made the use of the device in other economic areas inadvisable. Russian recognition of the fact that these mixed companies were not the best means for the regulation of economic relations between Socialist states came in 1947. According to Popovic, representatives of the U.S.S.R. during trade negotiations made the following statement: "Mixed companies are the appropriate formula for the cooperation with the dependent, but not with the independent and friendly countries." [9] Stalin agreed that a new start had to be made. He proposed to offer the Yugoslavs a credit of $135 million, to be used for the purchase of capital goods from the Soviet Union. Ultimately Yugoslavia received only $800,000 before the U.S.S.R. renounced the agreement in 1948.

Stalin's willingness to abandon the cruder forms of economic exploitation did not result, however, in an equally conciliatory attitude in other areas of concern to Yugoslavia. It is the judgment of the Yugoslavians and other less biased observers of history that by 1947 Stalin had decided to prepare for possible military conflict with the Western powers. With the founding of the Cominform in September 1947, the satellite dependencies lost what little freedom they had to travel their own roads to Socialism. Consolidation and integration of the camp was fostered not only in the economic and military areas, but in ideological questions as well. While the absorption of the satellites after 1945 had proceeded under the banner of People's Democracies—that is, coalition governments including all the "progressive elements"—the old formula was, after 1947, considered inadequate to the new demands of ideological unity. With monotonous unity, one after the other of the satellites now proclaimed that they were Dictatorships of the Proletariat on the Soviet model. By March 1948 Tito's resistance to the institutional and ideological recompression of the Soviet bloc seemed to Stalin to require further Soviet intervention. In the voluminous correspondence that passed between Moscow and Belgrade during the March-June period, the two countries discussed their difficulties with fraternal frankness. The problems of economic relations, of military advisers, and of the relations of a Socialist state to the "unified Socialist front" were discussed and rediscussed.

It is apparent from Yugoslavia's generally conciliatory attitude that she did not wish to see a rift about policy develop into a final breakdown of the solidarity of international Socialism. But her firm insistence on the right to develop Socialism in forms "somewhat different" from the social system in the U.S.S.R. provoked the Soviet Union into violent retaliatory language. To Yugoslavia's suggestion that its transformation might be of benefit to the revolutionary development in other countries and that its principles "are already being used," the Soviet Union responded with base name calling.

An unexpected feature of the dispute was the almost total absence of the ideological element. There were some critical references to Yugoslavia's use of the People's Front to unite majority support behind Tito's government. This merging of the Communist Party with non-party masses and the semi-legal status of the CPY did not appear to the Soviets to fulfill the requirements of the Dictatorship of the Proletariat. The accusation that Yugoslavia stubbornly refused to see significant theoretical differences between the U.S.S.R. and imperialist states had ideological overtones. But at this time, Tito's preference for a neutral position between the two blocs was not criticized as an abandonment of the traditional class struggle at the international level. Yugoslavia was warned, however, that the pursuit of "such a nationalist line" could only lead to Yugoslavia's degeneration into an ordinary bourgeois republic and to its transformation into a colony of the imperialist countries.

In June 1948 the Cominform expelled Yugoslavia and called on her people to help consolidate the united Socialist front against Imperialism, if need be, by replacing the current leaders of the CPY with a new leadership.

Though the resolution of June 1948 represented ostensibly the collective response of the Cominform to Yugoslavia's deviation, the frequency with which the dispute was discussed in terms of unresolved issues between the Soviet Union and Yugoslavia made it evident that both parties considered it a matter of bilateral relations.

If doubts remained, the official journal of the Cominform cleared them up in December 1948, by suggesting: "The attitude toward the Soviet Union is now the test of devotion to the cause of proletarian internationalism."

In sharp contrast to this view Tito, in a letter to the Central Committee of the CPSU, had told his Russian friends, "No matter how much each of us loves the land of Socialism, the U.S.S.R., he can, in no case, love his country less. . . ." The Yugoslavs, looking back on the 1948 crisis from the vantage point of a later date, showed considerable agreement about its cause: it was essentially the unresolved problem of the relations of Socialist countries to the Soviet Union that had produced the conflict.

Tito told his colleagues on the Central Committee of the CPY in 1948 ". . . remember that this is not . . . a question of errors committed by the CP of Yugoslavia. . . . The point here, first and foremost, is the relations between one state and another. It seems to me that they are using ideological questions in order to justify their pressure on us, on our state." [10] With the passing of Stalinism, new Soviet attempts were made to bring Yugoslavia back into the Socialist fold. An abject apology for past mistakes proffered by Khrushchev at Belgrade airport in 1955 made possible the Belgrade declaration and initiated a new period of good feeling. The 20th Congress of the CPUSSR, a year later, in accepting Yugoslavia's path as one of the four approved roads to Socialism, confirmed officially the correctness of Yugoslavia's original position.

However, the events in Hungary and Poland in the fall of the same year required a tightening of the ideological and political positions of the Socialist bloc. The new strictures on independent policies imposed by the Moscow Unity Declaration of 1957 provoked Yugoslavia's second defection from the Socialist Commonwealth. Tito's refusal to sign the 1957 document produced an initial wave of moderate comradely criticism. When, however, in the spring of 1958 the Yugoslav League of Communists approved a party program entitled "Yugoslavia's Way," their declaration of ideological independence initiated a new period of more vigorous criticism. The theoretical level of the second debate did not obscure the central fact: the issues in 1958 were the same that divided the Soviet bloc in 1948.

Yugoslavia, without success, attempted for the second time to avoid extensive discussion of ideological issues. Professions of faith in the essential principles of Socialism, of identity of aims, if not of practice, were met by dogmatic rejection. The joint efforts of the Soviet Union and China uncovered a long list of ideological deviations allegedly committed by Yugoslavia. The existence of a lengthy program, minutely detailing Yugoslavia's way to Socialism, offered an easy target. It also made the evasion of the discussion of ideological issues more difficult on Yugoslavia's part. The harrying tactics of Soviet and Chinese critics on ideological issues eventually induced Tito to assess the contemporary relevance of Marxism in terms which gave some semblance of truth to the Soviet-Chinese charge that Yugoslavia had largely abandoned Marxism: "Should we now, because of certain dogmatic interpretations of this science—and in the science and theory of Marxism and Leninism one can always find something that he may interpret in his own way, but this need not necessarily involve any essential points on which we may differ—give up our road to Socialism and our practice?" [11]

Tito's attempts to shift the debate to the political "core of this dispute," which for Yugoslavia remained "the question of relations between Socialist countries," were of no avail. Yugoslavia's repeated assertion that any acceptance on her part of the leading role of the Soviet Union within the Socialist world would only continue the "oppression of the weaker by the stronger," led Khrushchev to protest that only the insistence of other fraternal parties represented at the 1957 Moscow Conference had produced the formulation that appeared to assign a preferred position to the Soviet Union. Nevertheless, Yugoslavia remained unpersuaded. It was not difficult to recall that on earlier occasions Soviet theorists had argued that the existence of many Socialist countries would make it impossible to build Socialism in isolation. However unexceptionable in itself as a principle of Socialist cooperation at the international level, it led to a corollary principle for whose rejection Yugoslavia had been fighting since 1948: "Under certain conditions, proletarian inter-

nationalism demands the subordination of the interest of
the proletarian struggle in one country to the interests of
the struggle on a world wide basis." [12] To Yugoslavia,
formulas such as these represented "old forms of cooperation, stifling to the development of creative Socialism," and hence to be abandoned in favor of bilateral
relations. Indeed, the multilateral approach to the problem of relations between states of the 1957 Conference
was generally cited by Tito as the main reason for his
refusal to sign the Joint Declaration that emanated from
it. Yugoslavia's aversion to the multilateral approach
became apparent again in the discussion of economic relations between states. Here, also, the existence of regional
groupings and blocs was said to have introduced Capitalist concepts of exploitation into the economic relations
between Socialist states. "Considering the existing situation and the various negative traits of the existing regional groupings, Socialist Yugoslavia has not joined any
of them." [13] From the Soviet point of view the basic error
in Yugoslavia's analysis of relations between states could
be reduced to one proposition: it ignored the realities of
the class struggle. To stand aside, to ignore the family of
Socialist countries, to maintain neutrality under conditions of acute class struggle on a world-wide basis,
Khrushchev insisted, meant to "weaken the forces of the
revolutionary movement, the forces of Socialism, and
to aid the enemies of the working class." [14]

III

Even the most sketchy review of Soviet-Chinese Communist relations since 1949 reveals that the lessons
learned by the Soviet Union during the Yugoslav affair
were incorporated as soon as possible into Soviet policy
toward Communist China. Within twenty months following the death of Stalin, the Sino-Soviet accords of 1954
terminated such practices as had initially caused the Yugoslav-Soviet dispute. The Soviet Union agreed that her
military units were to be evacuated from Port Arthur. An
agreement was also reached to turn over to the Communist Chinese, for compensation, the Soviet share of the
four mixed companies which had been set up in 1950
and 1951. If there were any major conflicts between the
two countries in that period, they remained well con-

cealed. Perhaps the over-stressing on the part of Peking of the relevance of the Chinese Revolution to the social evolution of the colonial and semicolonial countries became a matter of minor annoyance to Moscow.[15] On one other question of a theoretical nature, division appeared possible. The acknowledged class nature of Communist China and the resultant unresolved contradictions that were said to exist in contemporary Chinese Communist society made it seem ideologically improper to Peking to label its regime a "Dictatorship of the Proletariat." By April 1956, however, the Soviet Union's persuasive insistence on ideological conformity had produced the desired change in verbal formulae.

Some two months earlier, the 20th Congress of the CPUSSR became the occasion for Soviet official acceptance of the Chinese path to Socialism.

The events in Hungary found Communist China occupying a position approximating that of Yugoslavia. The general approval of Soviet military intervention was tempered by a somewhat critical review of the Soviets' prior conduct toward her eastern European satellites. "Whatever had gone wrong in the relations between the Soviet Union and Hungary," the *People's Daily* said on November 21, "will be resolutely put right by the Soviet Union."

Toward Poland's lesser deviations, the Chinese Communists played the part of a benevolent critic. Their leaders apparently warned the Poles against trying to assume a role in international affairs outside the Socialist bloc. Nevertheless, the Poles gained the impression that their "Chinese friends fully understood," as the Polish Premier stated in welcoming Chou to Cracow in January 1957, that: ". . . the coexistence of nations should not be like the coexistence of various fish . . . living in one lake, the bigger devouring the smaller ones. We are fighting against all forms of national oppression." [16] The considerable frankness with which the events in Poland and particularly in Hungary were evaluated at this time by all members of the Communist community apparently did not make Chou believe that such unsubtle similes exceeded the bounds of ideological propriety. Whatever he may have said to his Polish friends in private, his public responses were entirely sympathetic. On his return trip

from Poland, the Premier of Communist China stopped
briefly in Moscow and signed on that occasion a joint
declaration in which the two countries attempted to
define, with some precision, the principles that were to
govern the future relations among Socialist countries. The
new formula, after the then-standard self-critical evaluation of the past in terms of "mistakes" and "shortcomings" and the usual emphasis on "complete equality" and
"non-interference in internal affairs," added one notable
principle: these relations of Socialist states—as defined
in part above—were to be "subordinated to supreme interests—those of victory in the common cause of struggle against imperialism, of victory in the cause of building
Socialism in different countries, of victory in the common
struggle for the triumph of Communism."

All the available evidence would seem to indicate that
the "rectification" campaign of February-June 1957, of
"letting a hundred flowers blossom and a hundred schools
of thought contend," should be interpreted as Communist
China's response to the events in Poland and Hungary. It
is of little significance here whether—internally—the hun-
dred-flower episode represented a genuine effort to "rectify the working style within the party," or whether its
true purpose was to make identification and political
"remolding" of the opposition more convenient. Chinese
Communist sources are not particularly helpful in this
matter. Lu-Ting-yi, alternate member of the Politbureau,
in July of 1960 while addressing the National Writers and
Artists Congress, supported both views. Whatever degree
of ambivalence the Communist regime had displayed
toward its internal critics during the early months of
1957, Premier Chou on June 26 converted the rectification campaign from an examination of party deficiencies
into a drive against rightists. The primary targets of the
initial attack were the prominent leaders of the non-
Communist captive parties represented in the coalition
government. In the main, the charges against them, particularly against the members of the so-called "Chang-Lo
Alliance" emphasized the close connection between the
eastern European crisis and the anti-rightist campaign.
Chang and Lo were accused of having contemplated the
seizure of state power, for "after the Hungarian affair
this clique considered that the Communist Party could

not continue leading the country, and that this offered the non-Communist parties their chance." [17]

The extent of the anti-rightist campaign can be estimated from the statement of the Chinese Communist leadership that within a month of its initiation more than one and one-third million counter-revolutionaries had been discovered. The official acknowledgment of the existence of such vast numbers of unregenerate bourgeois rightists within a Marxist society should not be considered as a contravention of the Marxist principle of the Dictatorship of the Proletariat. For, Marxism-Leninism as "creatively" applied in Communist China appears to permit for practical reasons the continued existence of two exploiting classes side by side with the two working classes. Because the bourgeoisie is said to possess a world outlook directly opposed to that of the Proletariat, antagonistic contradictions are generated which can be resolved only by a vigorous anti-rightist struggle. Since, in a theoretical sense, according to Chinese Communist writers "the question who wins has not been settled," periodic "Socialist revolutions" are necessary to maintain the balance of power in favor of the Proletariat. The anti-rightist struggles of 1957 and 1958 constituted such a revolution. The continuation of this campaign into 1959 as "the struggle against rightist opportunism" set a pattern not only for the internal policies of the regime in Communist China, but also shaped the international policies of Peking.

It is perhaps no more than a coincidence that during the week of June 22-29, 1957, the Central Committee of the CPSU considered the question of the so-called anti-party group, among whose members were Malenkov, Kaganovich, and Molotov. The long list of transgressions of which they were said to have been guilty included the following: they were "shackled by old notions," they were "dogmatic," they used a "scholastic inert approach," they were against "peaceful coexistence," etc., that is, in the accepted terminology of present-day Marxism, the Soviet anti-party group was guilty of Left-wing Dogmatism.

The adjustment of these antipodal theoretical problems that confronted the two main centers of Marxism was accomplished at the 1957 Moscow Meeting of Communist Parties. Leaning lightly to the Chinese Communist side, the parties unanimously agreed that: "In condemning dogmatism, the Communist Parties consider the main danger in present-day conditions to be revisionism or, in other words, right-wing opportunism, as a manifestation of bourgeois ideology that paralyzes the revolutionary energy of the working class and demands the preservation or restoration of Capitalism. However, dogmatism and sectarianism can also be the main danger at different stages of development of one party or another. Each Communist Party determines what danger is the main danger to it at a given time." In return for this endorsement of what constituted in effect Peking's point of view, Moscow was able to obtain recognition of its leading position in the Socialist camp.

The verbal disposition of the theoretical ingredient of conflict did not for long serve to eliminate complications in Soviet-Chinese Communist relations. In August 1958, the People's Commune program was initiated. On the occasion of its proclamation, the Chinese Communist Party's Central Committee also announced that the Commune system had brought the attainment of Communism within reach. In unequivocal language the Central Committee told the Chinese people that the goal of Communism would be reached within the proximate future. To the U.S.S.R. the theoretical implications of such assertions were of the greatest importance. Molotov had begun his long decline from the center of power in 1955 because of an overly pessimistic evaluation of the then-attained phase of Socialism in the Soviet Union. If 80- and 90-year-old peasants had a good chance to see the advent of Communism in China, as was suggested by the *Jen Min Jih Pao,* the Peking rulers had managed to surpass the social accomplishments of the Soviet Union. When, after Stalin's death in 1956, a similar claim had been advanced in the Soviet Union by some "hotheads" (to use Khrushchev's terminology), Khrushchev had firmly warned those people that this was not the moment to compile a detailed time table for the transition from Socialism to Communism. On the basis of such utopian views, Khrushchev explained, a negligent attitude toward the Socialist principle of material incentives had begun to take root.

The initial Soviet reaction to the Chinese claims was of an unofficial nature. In October 1958, *Voprosy philosophii* published an article which argued that the European Socialist countries, grouped into regions and united in a "community of mutual aid," would be the first to enter the final stage of Communism. The Asian Socialist countries, united into a second regional zone, would also achieve Communism jointly, but at a later date. The meaning was clear: even such minor European satellites as Albania and Bulgaria would reach Communism before Communist China.

In December 1958, the Central Committee of the Chinese Communist Party gave up some of the optimism of its earlier statement. It was now said officially, that it would take another 15 or 20 years for China to reach the stage of transition from Socialism to Communism, a stage that the Soviet Union had attained in the early 1950's. The depth of Soviet resentment of this whole episode may be gauged by the fact that, despite the Chinese recantation, in June 1960 *Pravda* referred to it again: "the contentions of the present-day leftists in the international Communist movement that, having power in one's hands, one may forthwith institute Communism, is erroneous and incorrect."

New disagreements of a theoretical nature began to arise at about the time Premier Khrushchev and President Eisenhower engaged in a bilateral attempt to settle outstanding international issues. Shortly after his trip to the United States in the fall of 1959, Khrushchev traveled to Peking, apparently to win China's support for the co-existence policy. Communist China had formally approved the "Spirit of Camp David," but, as the date of the projected Summit meeting approached, China's opposition to Khrushchev's foreign policy became more overt. In February 1960, during the meeting of the Warsaw Pact countries, the official observer of Communist China developed the main themes of China's dissent from Soviet external policies that have since caught the attention of the Western world. He gave notice to the Soviet Union and her European satellites that China's foreign policy would not be based upon compromises with Imperialism and that only its destruction by war could bring peace to the world. Peking's representative also suggested

that Socialism ought not to fear an atomic war, since the
Socialist camp would survive it and, indeed, as a consequence of war, Socialism would spread all over the
world. He added gratuitously that Communist China
would not be bound by any international agreements
made without her. By common consent, or on orders,
the Soviet Union and her European associates responded
to this presentation of the divergent Chinese point of
view in a manner that was to be employed again on later
occasions: the speech was not published in the Soviet or
Satellite press.[18]

The 90th anniversary of Lenin's birth in April 1960
was seized by Communist China as a suitable opportunity
to call once more for the forceful eradication of Imperialism. In addition to the arguments employed pre-
viously, there were now pointed references to attempts to
deceive Socialists about the nature of Imperialism. The
repeated use of Lenin's written works to back up Communist China's views about the nature of the enemy
made it apparent that the existing theoretical dispute
could only be resolved by the acceptance of Lenin's (that
is Communist China's) orthodox point of view. This im-
plication of possible revisionist tendencies in Moscow
made an exposition of the Soviet theoretical position
imperative. The impressive instrument chosen to repel
the Chinese attack was Mr. Kuusinen, member of the
Politburo and one of the few surviving associates of
Lenin. Like other later defenders of the Soviet point of
view Mr. Kuusinen was confronted by the embarrassing
difficulty that Lenin had not endorsed peaceful coexistence in a manner that would provide suitable quotations.
Nevertheless, over a period of some months during the
summer of 1960, the Soviet policy of peaceful coexistence
was resolutely defended against all attacks from Chinese
sources. It is not necessary here to trace minor theoretical divergences that emerged in this dispute between
Communist China and the Soviet Union, such as the nature of the transition to Socialism. It is also superfluous
to define the areas of ideological compatibilities: they
were both hostile to Revisionism, particularly on the
Yugoslav model.

Three principal issues divided them at the theoretical
level: (1) the possibility of coexistence with Imperialism;

(2) the effects of thermonuclear war on the two world systems; and (3) the propriety of temporary compromises with the common enemy.

The revival of the coexistence policy—it had been used briefly during the 1920's—is a relatively recent development intimately associated with Khrushchev's rise to power. As recently as 1954 he maintained essentially Stalin's old thesis of "Capitalist encirclement." In 1956, when the 20th Congress of the Russian Communist Party was asked to endorse formally the concept of peaceful coexistence, Khrushchev presented the issue with a good deal of equivocation. Two years later, however, the old principle of Capitalist encirclement was abandoned by the Soviet Premier, when he said: "I would like to draw your attention to the fact that at present the concept of 'capitalist encirclement' of our country itself seriously needs a more accurate definition. With the formation of the world system of Socialism the situation of the world has altered radically and it has not altered . . . to the advantage of Capitalism. At present it is not known who encircles whom." [19]

At the 21st Congress of the CPSU in 1959 Khrushchev declared with finality: "Capitalist encirclement of our country no longer exists. There are two world social systems: Capitalism which is coming to the end of its days, and Socialism in the full flood of its growing forces. . . ." Khrushchev appeared to argue that whatever capabilities Capitalism might still possess, they would within the proximate future be reduced to a minimum, given the appropriate policy on the part of the Socialist forces, i.e., peaceful coexistence.

The Chinese Communists have been a good deal more pessimistic in their evaluation of the prospects of Capitalistic decay. Just as from the beginning of the 1870's there prevailed a period of peaceful development of Capitalism, so now there exists "a kind of domestic peace" in many Capitalist countries. In this atmosphere revisionist trends find it easy to grow and spread. The Chinese were particularly disturbed by, and they warned against, the abandonment of the class approach in fundamental questions of foreign policy. Repudiation of the class approach, it was argued, would impede the development of the class struggle in the Capitalist countries and the development of the national-liberation movement. Such arguments, countered *Pravda*, "are the fruit of an unwillingness to understand the essence of the principle of peaceful coexistence. The principle is none other than the highest form of the class struggle between two opposing systems." [20]

The acrimonious tone of the debate was maintained in the discussion of the inevitability and consequences of war. Peking persisted in its oft-repeated view that: "Until the Imperialist system and the exploiting classes come to an end, wars of one kind or another will always appear. And the result will certainly not be the annihilation of mankind. On the debris of dead Imperialism, the victorious people would create with extreme rapidity a civilization thousands of times higher than the Capitalist system." [21] *Pravda* answered as follows: "In modern conditions the emergence of views similar to those of the 'left' Communists could only play into the hands of the Imperialists by helping them spread false tales of 'aggressive Communism.' The emergence of such left-sectarian views could only have a demoralizing influence on the builders of the new society. Why . . . build and create if you know ahead of time that all the fruits of your labor will be destroyed by the scourge of war? These views have nothing in common with Communism." [22]

In attacking the policy of compromise the Chinese Communists also expressed concern about "a certain lowering of theoretical standards." The history of the Chinese Communist Party furnished a relevant example. In 1927, Chen Tu-hsiu's opportunism led the party into the united front with the Kuomintang. The result was defeat for the revolution.

On the 40th anniversary of the publication of Lenin's book, *Left Wing Communism: An Infantile Disorder*, *Pravda* published an extensive review of the work, whose title by itself stood for a rejection of the Chinese ideological position. "Naïve and completely inexperienced people," Lenin was quoted as having written, "imagine that it is only necessary to concede the admissibility of compromises *at all* and any dividing line will be erased between opportunism, with which we are conducting and must conduct an implacable struggle, and revolutionary Marxism or Communism." [23]

The deepening division between the Soviet Union and Communist China demanded remedial measures. In November 1960, the mediatory efforts of the 81-Nation Moscow Conference succeeded in preserving the façade of Socialist unity. From the Soviet point of view, the price of unity was not inconsiderable. The Chinese theory prevailed that wars of national liberation deserved the active support of Socialist states. Furthermore, the willingness of the Soviet Union to have differences of a theoretical nature arbitrated before an international forum implied, in effect, the acceptance of a polycentered Socialist camp. Khrushchev's attempt to dispose of the "Albanian Issue" unilaterally, at the 22nd national Congress of the CPSU, consequently, not only met the determined resistance of the Albanians, but also reopened the controversy between Communist China and the Soviet Union.

IV

The given frame of reference of this introduction has made it possible to evaluate the stresses and strains within the Communist bloc as if bloc affairs followed patterns of their own, totally unaffected by outside influences.

Such obviously is not the case. The image of the non-Communist world is of crucial importance to the fashioning of Socialist bloc policies. Identification of enemies or the members of the neutral camp presents no particular difficulty. A common goal is shared by all. Consequently, the search for the significance of such disagreements as reach the level of public argument inevitably leads to a discussion of means to attain the shared goal. But more is involved here than an academic discussion about revolutionary tactics and techniques.

To use Marxist terminology: the Mode of Production shapes the superstructure, that is, the uneven development of the three independent centers of the Communist bloc produces separate national interests and policies. The Soviet Union's path to Socialism centers on the concept of peaceful competition with Capitalism. Khrushchev's way would seem to require a prolonged period of international relaxation in order to devote all available capital resources to the broadening of the Soviet economic base that would assure—first in the economic and then in the political area—the victory of Socialism over Capitalism.

The ultimate victory, even if postponed beyond the present decade, would seem to depend upon the perfect interaction of all the constituent parts of the Master Plan as developed at the 22nd Congress.

In the People's Republic of China, Mao Tse-tung leads a political society still structured on a class basis. But the overcoming of internal resistance represents only a part of the effort to live up to the design of the future. The internal generation of capital resources adequate to fulfill the promise of plenty requires, as Tito put it, the application of "inhuman" measures for a prolonged period of time. The inability to meet interim economic targets is compounded by the frustrations of political plans and goals. While fraternal assistance has been available in terms of credits, it has not been sufficiently large and it has meant dependency not compatible with great-power status. The creation of the image of a hostile world confronting China furnishes a means of spurring the indigenous population to greater effort, explains the sharp repression of internal opposition, and—as a corollary—encourages extreme ideological orthodoxy. But orthodoxy has a tendency to degenerate into dogmatism. And in a Socialist Commonwealth where the truth emerges from more than one source, dogmatism leads to conflict. Thus, the sharpened picture of the class struggle at the international level drawn by Chinese sources cannot possibly be accommodated to the principles of peaceful coexistence advocated by Khrushchev.

Little need be said about Tito. The violence of the Russian and Chinese attacks against Yugoslav revisionism attests to the latter's success. The Yugoslavs, as good Marxists, also employ ideology as the medium through which one views the world. The central theme that emerges is that of the gradual evolution of the world toward Socialism. Since its victory is certain, there is much less preoccupation with the evaluation of means to assure the inevitable.

This perusal of the genesis of strained imperial relations in the Socialist commonwealth represents a measure of the task that confronts Khrushchev and his associates. Persistent strains are not merely as annoying as is a poor harvest in Kazakhstan, but may prove fatal to Khrushchev's path to Communism both in a national and personal sense.

The attempt in 1955 to wipe clean the slate in Yugoslav-Soviet relations with an abject apology for the past mistakes of others did not produce lasting improvements. Conciliatory gestures produce new demands, based upon imagined or real national interests. Eventually they have to be resisted. The cyclical pattern is repeated until the point is reached where the conflicting national interests can only be adjusted, for the sake of preserving the unity of the Socialist bloc, by the subordination—albeit temporary—of all national interests to the cause of unity.

The 1957 Unity Declaration of Communist Parties represented such an attempt. But it remained unsigned by Yugoslavia and produced a counter-declaration in "Yugoslavia's Way" a year later, and China's interpretation of it after 1959 deviated considerably from that of the Soviet Union. Attempts to paper over renewed disagreements in 1960 and 1961 were no more successful.

Fraternal criticism soon degenerates into ideological name-calling. Ideological disunity produces disunity in policies that may re-enforce existing centrifugal tendencies to the point where the notion of a viable Moscow-centered Socialist camp can safely be laid aside.

NOTES

1. *Kommunist,* October 8, 1955
2. Central Committee CPSU Resolution, November 2, 1957
3. Central Committee CPSU Resolution, June 29, 1957
4. The London *Times* December 18, 1958
5. Cf. Part III
6. Joseph Stalin, *Foundations of Leninism,* Revised translation, New York, 1932, p. 23
7. New York *Times,* August 5, 1959
8. Popovic, M., *On Economic Relations among Socialist States,* London, 1950, p. 68
9. *Ibid.,* p. 63
10. Dedijer, V., *Tito,* New York, 1953, p. 338
11. From Tito's Speech, made November 23, 1958; *Yugoslav Facts and Views,* No. 73
12. Baas, R. and Marbury, E., *The Soviet Yugoslav Controversy,* 1948-1958, New York, 1959, p. 159

13. *Yugoslavia's Way,* trans. Stoyan Pribechvich, New York, 1958, p. 74

14. From Khrushchev's Speech, July 11, 1958; *Current Digest of the Soviet Press,* Vol. 10, No. 28

15. Boorman, H. L., *et al., Moscow-Peking Axis,* New York, 1957, p. 43

16. New York *Times,* January 15, 1957

17. *Tensions in Communist China,* Senate Document No. 66, 86th Congress, 1st Session

18. Yowev, S., "Die Ideologischen Gegensaetze Zwischen Chruschtschow and Mao Tse-tung," *Aus Politik und Zeitgeschichte,* 29. Juni, 1960

19. *Khrushchev on the Shifting Balance of World Forces,* Senate Document No. 57, 86th Congress, 1st Session

20. *Pravda,* August 12, 1960; *Current Digest of the Soviet Press,* Vol. 12, No. 32

21. Cf. Part V, "Long Live Leninism"

22. *Pravda,* August 7, 1960; *Current Digest of the Soviet Press,* Vol. 12, No. 32

23. *Pravda,* June 12, 1960; *Current Digest of the Soviet Press,* Vol. 12, No. 24

Part I

The 20th Congress of the C.P.S.U.: The Redefinition of Doctrine

The year 1955 saw a good many efforts on the part of the Soviet Union to divest itself of the Stalinist heritage: the Cold War with the West was temporarily replaced by the Spirit of Geneva, relations with Tito were put aright with suitable apologies for the mistakes of the Stalinist period, and a determined attempt was made to increase the area of friendly contacts with important Asian states.

In internal affairs the demotion of Malenkov and Molotov also served to emphasize that advocates of old theories had lost the right to participate prominently in the formulation of Soviet policies. The success of these endeavors to make a clean break with the past encouraged Khrushchev to use the forum of the 20th Congress of the C.P.S.U. to present a basic exposition of the principles that would guide future Soviet international policy. To the West Khrushchev offered peaceful competition and the thesis that war might not be inevitable. National liberation movements were promised both the end of colonialism and Soviet economic aid without strings, and the associates in the Socialist camp received official approval of separate roads to Socialism.

— 1 —

EXCERPT FROM KHRUSHCHEV'S REPORT TO THE 20TH PARTY CONGRESS

February, 1956*

SOME FUNDAMENTAL QUESTIONS OF PRESENT-DAY INTERNATIONAL DEVELOPMENT

Comrades! I should like to dwell on some fundamental questions concerning present-day international development which determine not only the present course of events but also future prospects.

These are the questions of peaceful coexistence of the two systems, the possibility of preventing wars in the present era, and the forms of transition to socialism in different countries.

Let us examine these questions briefly.

The peaceful coexistence of the two systems. The Leninist principle of peaceful coexistence of states with different social systems has always been and remains the general line of our country's foreign policy.

It has been alleged that the Soviet Union advances the principle of peaceful coexistence merely out of tactical considerations, considerations of expediency. Yet it is common knowledge that we have always, from the very

* *The Current Digest of the Soviet Press,* Vol. VIII, No. 4, 1956, published weekly at Columbia University by the Joint Committee on Slavic Studies appointed by the American Council of Learned Societies and the Social Science Research Council. Reprinted by permission.

first years of Soviet power, stood with equal firmness for peaceful coexistence. Hence it is not a tactical move, but a fundamental principle of Soviet foreign policy.

This means that, if there is indeed a threat to the peaceful coexistence of countries with differing social-political systems, it by no means comes from the Soviet Union or the socialist camp. . . .

To this day, the enemies of peace allege that the Soviet Union is out to overthrow capitalism in other countries by "exporting" revolution. It goes without saying that among us Communists there are no supporters of capitalism. But this does not at all mean that we have interfered or plan to interfere in the internal affairs of countries where the capitalists order exists. . . . It is ridiculous to think that revolutions are made to order. One often hears representatives of bourgeois countries reasoning thus: "The Soviet leaders claim that they are for peaceful coexistence between the two systems. At the same time, they declare that they are fighting for Communism and say that communism is bound to win in all countries. How can there be any peaceful coexistence with the Soviet Union if it is fighting for communism?" This interpretation is formed under the influence of bourgeois propaganda. The ideologists of the bourgeoisie, distorting the facts, deliberately confuse questions of ideological struggle with questions of relations between states in order to make the Communists of the Soviet Union seem aggressive people.

When we say that the socialist system will win in the competition between the two systems—the capitalist and the socialist—this by no means signifies that its victory will be achieved through armed interference by the socialist countries in the internal affairs of capitalist countries. Our certainty of the victory of communism is based on the fact that the socialist mode of production possesses decisive superiority over the capitalist mode of production. Precisely because of this, the ideas of Marxism-Leninism are more and more capturing the minds of the broad masses of the working people in the capitalist countries, just as they have captured the minds of millions of men and women in our country and the people's democracies.

We believe that all the working people on earth, once

they have become convinced of the advantages communism brings, will sooner or later take the road of struggle for the construction of a socialist society. Building communism in our country, we are resolutely against war. We have always held and continue to hold that the establishment of a new social system in one or another country is the internal affair of the peoples of the countries concerned. This is our position, based on the great Marxist-Leninist teaching. The principle of peaceful coexistence is gaining ever wider international recognition. This principle has become one of the cornerstones of the foreign policy of the Chinese People's Republic and the other people's democracies. It is being actively implemented by the Republic of India, the Union of Burma, and a number of other countries. And this is natural, for there is no other way in present-day conditions. Indeed, there are only two ways: either peaceful coexistence or the most destructive war in history. There is no third way.

We believe that countries with differing social systems can do more than exist side by side. It is necessary to proceed further, to improve relations, strengthen confidence among countries and cooperate. The historic significance of the famous five principles, advanced by the Chinese People's Republic and the Republic of India and supported by the Bandung Conference and the broad world public, is that in today's circumstances they provide the best form for relations among countries with different social systems. Why not make these principles the foundation of peaceful relations among all countries in all parts of the world? It would meet the vital interests and demands of the peoples if all countries subscribed to the five principles.

The possibility of preventing war in the present era. Millions of people all over the world are asking whether another war is really inevitable, whether mankind, which has already experienced two devastating world wars, must go through still a third one. Marxists must answer this question, taking into consideration the epoch-making changes of the last decades.

As we know, there is a Marxist-Leninist precept that wars are inevitable as long as imperialism exists. This thesis was evolved at a time when (1) imperialism was

n all-embracing world system and (2) the social and
political forces which did not want war were weak, in-
sufficiently organized, and hence unable to compel the
imperialists to renounce war.

People usually take only one aspect of the question;
they consider only the economic basis of wars under imperialism. This is not enough. War is not only an economic phenomenon. Whether there is to be a war or not
depends in large measure on the correlation of class,
political forces, the degree of organization and the awareness and resolve of the people. In certain conditions,
moreover, the struggle waged by progressive social and
political forces can play a decisive role. Hitherto the
state of affairs was such that the forces that did not want
war and came out against it were poorly organized and
lacked the means to oppose their will to the schemes of
the warmakers. Thus it was before World War I, when
the main force fighting the threat of war—the world
proletariat—was disorganized by the betrayal by the
leaders of the Second International. Thus it was on the
eve of World War II, too, when the Soviet Union was
the only country pursuing an active peace policy; when
the other great powers to all intents and purposes encouraged the aggressors, and the right-wing Social-Democratic leaders had split the workers' movement in the
capitalist countries.

For that period, the above-mentioned thesis was absolutely correct. At the present time, however, the situation has changed radically. Now there is a world camp
of socialism which has become a mighty force. In this
camp the peace forces have not only the moral but also
the material means to prevent aggression. There is a large
group of other countries, moreover, with a population
running into many hundreds of millions, which is actively working to avert war. The workers' movement in
the capitalist countries has become a tremendous force
today. The movement of peace supporters has sprung up
and developed into a powerful factor.

In these circumstances, of course, the Leninist thesis remains valid: As long as imperialism exists, the economic
base giving rise to wars will also remain. That is why we
must display the greatest vigilance. As long as capitalism
survives in the world, reactionary forces, representing the

interests of the capitalist monopolies, will continue the
drive toward military gambles and aggression and ma
try to unleash war. But war is not a fatalistic inev
tability. Today there are mighty social and political force
possessing formidable means to prevent the imperialis
from unleashing war and, if they try to start it, to give
smashing rebuff to the aggressors and frustrate their ad
venturist plans. For this it is necessary for all anti-wa
forces to be vigilant and mobilized; they must act as
united front and not relax their efforts in the struggle fo
peace. The more actively the peoples defend peace, th
greater the guarantee that there will be no new war.

Forms of transition to socialism in different countrie:
In connection with the radical changes in the worl
arena, new prospects are also opening up in regard to th
transition of countries and nations to socialism.

As far back as on the eve of the great October socia
ist revolution, V. I. Lenin wrote: "All nations will a
rive at socialism—this is inevitable—but not all will d
so in exactly the same way. Each will contribute some
thing of its own in one or another form of democracy
one or another variety of the dictatorship of the prole
tariat, one or another rate at which socialist transforma
tions will be effected in the various aspects of socia
life. . . ."

Historical experience has fully confirmed this bri
liant precept of Lenin's. Now, alongside the Soviet forn
of reorganizing society on socialist foundations, we hav
the form of people's democracy.

This form sprang up in Poland, Bulgaria, Czechoslov:
kia, Albania, and the other European people's democr:
cies and is being employed in conformity with the specifi
historical, social and economic conditions and peculiar
ties of each of these countries. It has been thorough!
tried and tested for ten years and has fully proved i
worth.

Much that is unique in socialist construction is bein
contributed by the Chinese People's Republic, possessir
an economy which was exceedingly backward and bore
semi-feudal and semicolonial character until the triump
of the revolution. Having taken over the decisive con
manding positions, the people's democratic state is pu

uing a policy of peaceful reorganization for private industry and trade and their gradual transformation into components of the socialist economy in the course of the socialist revolution.

Leadership of the great cause of socialist reconstruction by the Communist Party of China and the Communist and Workers' Parties of the other people's democracies in keeping with the peculiarities and specific features of each country is creative Marxism in action. In the Federal People's Republic of Yugoslavia, where power belongs to the working people and society is founded on public ownership of the means of production, unique specific forms of economic management and organization of the state apparatus are arising in the process of socialist construction.

It is quite probable that the forms of transition to socialism will become more and more varied; moreover, achieving these forms need not be associated with civil war under all circumstances. Our enemies like to depict us Leninists as advocates of violence always and everywhere. True, we recognize the need for the revolutionary transformation of capitalist society into socialist society. It is this that distinguishes the revolutionary Marxists from the reformists, the opportunists. There is no doubt that in a number of capitalist countries violent overthrow of the dictatorship of the bourgeoisie and the sharp aggravation of class struggle connected with this are inevitable. But the forms of social revolution vary. And it is not true that we regard violence and civil war as the only way to remake society. . . .

Leninism teaches that the ruling classes do not surrender power voluntarily. However, the greater or lesser intensity which the struggle may assume, the use or nonuse of violence in the transition to socialism depend on the resistance of the exploiters, on whether the exploiting class itself resorts to violence, rather than on the proletariat.

In this connection the question arises of whether it is possible to go over to socialism by using parliamentary means. No such course was open to the Russian Bolsheviks, who were the first to effect this transition. Lenin showed us another road—that of the establishment of a

republic of Soviets, the only correct road in those historical conditions. Following that course, we achieved a
world-historic victory.

Since then, however, the historical situation has un-
dergone radical changes which make possible a new approach to the question. The forces of socialism and democracy have grown immeasurably throughout the world
and capitalism has become much weaker. The mighty
camp of socialism, with its population of over 900,000,-
000 is growing and gaining in strength. Its huge interna-
forces, its decisive advantages over capitalism are being
increasingly revealed from day to day. Socialism has a
great power of attraction for the workers, peasants and
intellectuals of all countries. The ideas of socialism are
indeed, coming to dominate the minds of all toiling humanity.

At the same time, in present-day conditions the working class in many capitalist countries has a genuine opportunity to unite the overwhelming majority of the people under its leadership and to ensure that the basic
means of production are placed in the hands of the people. Right bourgeois parties and the governments which
they form are suffering failure more and more often. In
these conditions, the working class, uniting around itself
the working peasantry, the intellectuals and all patriotic
forces, and firmly rebuffing opportunist elements incapable of renouncing a policy of collaboration with the capitalists and landlords, has an opportunity to defeat the reactionary, antipopular forces, to win a firm majority in
parliament and to turn the parliament from an agency of
bourgeois democracy into an instrument of genuinely
popular will. In such a case this institution, traditional in
many highly developed capitalist countries, may become
an agency of genuine democracy, of democracy for the
working people.

The winning of a firm parliamentary majority based
on the mass revolutionary movement of the proletariat
and of the working people would create conditions for
the working class of many capitalist and formerly colonial
countries to make fundamental social changes.

Of course, in those countries where capitalism is still
strong, where it possesses a tremendous military and po-
lice machine, serious resistance by reactionary forces is

inevitable. The transition to socialism in these countries will take place amid sharp revolutionary class struggle.

In all the forms of transition to socialism, an absolute and decisive requirement is political leadership of the working class, headed by its vanguard. The transition to socialism is impossible without this.

It is necessary to emphasize strongly that the more favorable conditions for the triumph of socialism in other countries have arisen because socialism triumphed in the Soviet Union and is winning in the people's democracies. And our victory would have been impossible if Lenin and the party of the Bolsheviks had not championed revolutionary Marxism against the reformists who broke with Marxism and took the road of opportunism.

Such are the considerations which the Party Central Committee considers necessary to present on the question of the forms of transition to socialism in present-day conditions.

Part II

Experiments in Separate Roads to Socialism: National Communism and Revolution

The Yugoslav-Soviet Declaration of June 1956 reiterated the Soviet attitude of tolerance toward separate roads to Socialism. Within a week the Poznan riots had occurred. In the Fall of 1956 further proof was offered that the new definition of permissible limits of deviation had encouraged in Poland and Hungary a version of national Communism and finally separatism, requiring Soviet intervention to prevent defection of the two states from the Socialist camp. The explanation of Soviet military intervention in Hungary, though stressing primarily Moscow's responsibility to end the counterrevolution in that country, also conceded that Soviet conduct had contributed to the deterioriation of relations between Moscow and the satellites. But again, a sharp distinction was made between admittedly incorrect Soviet conduct prior to 1956, and the entire correctness of the new policies approved by the 20th Congress.

Chinese and Yugoslav comment on the Polish and particularly the Hungarian affair combined a reluctant approval of Soviet intervention with a frank condemnation of the Soviets' share in the difficulties within and with the East European satellites.

The initial Chinese and Yugoslav criticism of Soviet past policies toward the other members of the Socialist camp showed much agreement. Tito's subsequent statement that remnants of the Stalinist system had survived their explicit condemnation at the 20th Congress persuaded the Chinese to adopt a more active supporting role of the Soviets. But the joint attack on the improprie-

ties of the Yugoslav position, specifically on the Hungarian debacle, and more generally as regards her attitude toward the Socialist camp, revealed significant differences in the Soviet and Chinese analysis of the Yugoslav deviation. For the Soviets, the denigration of Stalin at the 20th Congress made it difficult to attack Yugoslav anti-Stalinism. Hence, Yugoslavia is accused of national communism, of an overbearing assessment of her own contribution to the evolution of Socialism, of an improper attack on the fraternal Albanian Party. For the Chinese, unburdened by a commitment to Khrushchev's "secret" speech, total condemnation of Stalinism now became equated with Revisionism, with giving aid and comfort to the common enemy, Capitalism.

— 2 —

DECLARATION ON RELATIONS BETWEEN THE COMMUNIST PARTIES OF THE U.S.S.R. AND YUGOSLAVIA

June 20, 1956*

The Belgrade Declaration of June 2, 1955, placed the relations between the two Socialist countries on sound foundations, and the principles made public in it are finding ever broader application in their mutual cooperation. . . .

Abiding by the view that the roads and conditions of Socialist development are different in different countries, that the wealth of the forms of Socialist development contributes to their strengthening, and starting with the fact that any tendency of imposing one's own views in determining the roads and forms of Socialist development are alien to both sides, the two sides have agreed that the foregoing cooperation should be based on complete freedom of will and equality, on friendly criticism and on the comradely character of the exchange of views on disputes between our parties.

Placed on the mentioned foundations, cooperation between the League of Communists of Yugoslavia and the Communist Party of the Soviet Union will evolve primarily along the way of a comprehensive mutual study of the forms and methods of Socialist development in the two countries, the free and comradely exchange of ex-

* New York *Times,* June 21, 1956. Reprinted by permission.

periences and views on questions of general interest for the development of Socialist practice and the promotion of Socialist thought, and also on questions relating to peace, rapprochement and linking up between nations and the progress of mankind in general.

— 3 —

SOVIET STATEMENT ON TIES TO THE SATELLITES
October 30, 1956*

The principles of peaceful coexistence, friendship and cooperation among all states have always been and still form the unshakable foundation of the external relations of the U.S.S.R. This policy finds its most profound and consistent expression in the relationship with Socialist countries.

United by the common ideal of building a Socialist society and the principles of proletarian internationalism, countries of the great commonwealth of Socialist nations can build their relations only on the principle of full equality, respect of territorial integrity, state independence and sovereignty and non-interference in the domestic affairs of one another.

This not only does not exclude, but on the contrary presupposes close fraternal cooperation and mutual aid between the countries of the Socialist commonwealth in the economic, political and cultural spheres. It was on this basis that, after the second World War and the rout of fascism there, the regimes of the Peoples Democracy came into being in a number of countries of Europe and Asia, strengthened and displaying great vitality.

In the process of the establishment of the new regime

* New York *Times,* October 31, 1956. Reprinted by permission.

and the deep revolutionary transformation in social relations there were not a few difficulties, unsolved problems and downright mistakes, including those in the relations between the Socialist states, violations and mistakes which infringed the principles of equality in relations between Socialist states.

The Twentieth Congress of the Communist party of the Soviet Union resolutely condemned these mistakes and violations and demanded that the Soviet Union should apply (Lenin's) principles of equality of nations in her relations with other Socialist states. This statement fully took into account the historical past and the peculiarities of each country which has taken the road of building a new life.

The Soviet Government is consistently putting into practice these historic decisions of the Twentieth Congress, which create conditions for the further strengthening of friendship and cooperation between Socialist countries and the inviolable basis of maintaining the complete sovereignty of every Socialist state. . . .

The Soviet Government regards it as indispensable to make a statement in connection with the events in Hungary.

The course of events has shown that the working people of Hungary, who achieved great progress on the basis of the people's democratic order, are rightly raising the question of the necessity of eliminating serious shortcomings in the field of economic building, of the further raising of the material well-being of the population and of the struggle against bureaucratic distortions in the state apparatus.

However, this just and progressive movement of the working people was soon joined by forces of the black reaction and counter-revolution, which are trying to take advantage of the discontent on the part of the working people in order to undermine the foundations of the people's democratic order in Hungary and to restore there the old landlords' and capitalists' orders.

The Soviet Government, like the whole of the Soviet people, deeply regret that the development of events in Hungary has led to bloodshed. At the request of the Hungarian People's Government, the Soviet Government consented to the entry into Budapest of Soviet Army units for the purpose of assisting the Hungarian People's Army and the Hungarian organs of authority to establish order in the town.

Since it considers that the further presence of Soviet Army units in Hungary can serve as a cause for an even greater deterioration of the situation, the Soviet Government has given an instruction to its military command to withdraw the Soviet Army units from Budapest as soon as this is recognized by the Hungarian Government to be necessary.

At the same time, the Soviet Government is ready to enter into corresponding negotiations with the Government of the Hungarian People's Republic and other participants of the Warsaw Treaty on the question of the presence of Soviet troops on the territory of Hungary.

The defense of Socialist achievements by People's Democratic Hungary is at the present moment the chief and sacred duty of workers, peasants and intelligentsia, and of the whole toiling Hungarian people.

The Soviet Government expresses the confidence that the peoples of the Socialist countries will not permit foreign and internal reactionary forces to undermine the basis of the People's Democratic regime, won and consolidated by the heroic struggle and toil of the workers, peasants and intelligentsia of each country.

They will make all efforts to remove all obstacles that lie in the path of further strengthening the democratic basis of the independence and sovereignty of their countries, to develop further the Socialist basis of each country, their economy and culture for the sake of the constant growth of the material welfare and the cultural level of all the workers. They will consolidate the fraternal unity and mutual assistance of the Socialist countries for the strengthening of the great cause of peace and socialism.

CHINESE GOVERNMENT STATEMENT ON THE SOVIET DECLARATION

November 1, 1956*

The Government of the Soviet Union on October 30, 1956, issued a declaration on the foundations of the development and further strengthening of friendship and cooperation between the Soviet Union and other socialist countries. The Government of the People's Republic of China considers this declaration of the Government of the Soviet Union to be correct. This declaration is of great importance in correcting errors in mutual relations between the socialist countries and in strengthening unity among them.

The People's Republic maintains that the five principles of mutual respect for sovereignty and territorial integrity, non-aggression, non-intervention in each other's internal affairs, equality and mutual benefit, and peaceful coexistence should be the principles governing the establishment and development of mutual relations among the nations of the world. The socialist countries are all independent, sovereign states. At the same time they are united by the common ideal of socialism and the spirit of proletarian internationalism. Consequently, mutual relations between socialist countries all the more so should be established on the basis of these five principles. Only in this way are the socialist countries able to achieve genuine fraternal friendship and solidarity and through mutual assistance and cooperation, their desire for a mutual economic upsurge. As the declaration of the Soviet Government pointed out, the mutual relations between the socialist countries are not without mistakes. These

* *Survey of China Mainland Press,* Bulletin No. 1405, November 6, 1956.

mistakes resulted in estrangement and misunderstandings between certain socialist countries. Some of these countries have been unable to build socialism better in accordance with their historical circumstances and special features because of these mistakes. As a result of these estrangements and misunderstandings, a tense situation has sometimes occurred which otherwise would not have occurred. The handling of the 1948-1949 Yugoslav situation and the recent happenings in Poland are enough to illustrate this. Following the Soviet-Yugoslav joint declaration issued in June 1955, the Soviet Government has again taken note of this problem and in its declaration of October 30, 1956, indicated its willingness to solve various problems in mutual relations on the basis of the principles of full equality, respect for territorial integrity, national independence and sovereignty, and non-intervention in each other's internal affairs and by friendly negotiations with other socialist countries. This important step is clearly of value in eliminating estrangement and misunderstandings among the socialist countries. It will help increase their friendship and cooperation.

The Government of the People's Republic of China notes that the people of Poland and Hungary in the recent happenings have raised demands that democracy, independence, and equality be strengthened and the material well-being of the people be raised on the basis of developing production. These demands are completely proper. Correct satisfaction of these demands is not only helpful to consolidation of the people's democratic system in these countries but also favorable to the unity among the socialist countries. We consider it absolutely necessary to take note of this and to differentiate between the just demands of the broadest mass of the people and the conspiratorial activities of an extremely small number of reactionary elements. The question of uniting the broadest mass of the people in the struggle against an extremely small number of reactionary elements is not only a question for an individual socialist country, but one deserving attention by many socialist countries, including our country.

Because of the unanimity of ideology and aim of struggle, it often happens that certain personnel of socialist countries neglect the principle of equality among nations in their mutual relations. Such a mistake, by nature, is the error of bourgeois chauvinism. Such a mistake, particularly the mistake of chauvinism by a big country, inevitably results in serious damage to the solidarity and common cause of the socialist countries. For this reason, leading members and personnel of our government and the people of the entire country, must at all times be vigilant to prevent the error of big nation chauvinism in relations with socialist countries and others. We should at all times carry out education resolutely to oppose big nation chauvinism among our personnel and the people of the entire country. If such an error is committed it should be corrected promptly. This is the duty to which we should pay the utmost attention in order to strive for peaceful coexistence with all nations and to promote the cause of world peace.

— 5 —

ADDRESS BY TITO BEFORE A MEETING OF THE YUGOSLAV LEAGUE OF COMMUNISTS
Pula—November 11, 1956

. . . You know, in the main, what causes brought about the events in Poland and Hungary. We must go back to 1948 when Yugoslavia was the first to give an energetic answer to Stalin and declared that it wanted to be independent, that it wanted to build its life and socialism in accordance with the specific conditions of the country, and that it allowed no one to interfere in its internal affairs.

Materially, no armed intervention took place then because Yugoslavia was united. Because we liquidated their main force during the national liberation war, various reactionary elements were unable to carry out various provocations.

Secondly, we had a very strong, united and monolithic Communist Party, hardened during the prewar period and during the national liberation struggle. We had also a strong and steeled Army, and, what is most important, we had a unity of the people which characterized all that.

When the truth about our country prevailed, and the period of normalization of relations with the countries which broke their relations with us following the ill-renowned resolution began, the leaders of the Eastern countries expressed their desire that we should no longer mention what had been done against us, that we should forget what had been done. We accepted that, only to improve our relations with these countries as soon as possible.

But you will see later that it is most necessary to remind certain people, who are today again beginning to slander our country and who are at the head of the Communist parties in the Eastern countries and also in certain Western countries, of what they did against Yugoslavia during those four, five and more years when Yugoslavia stood quite alone face to face against an enormous propaganda apparatus, when we had to fight on all sides to preserve the achievements of our national revolution, to preserve what we had already started building, that is, the foundations of socialism—briefly, to wipe away the infamy which they wanted to put on us by various slanders, and to show where the truth was.

We must remind them and say that then those same people accused our country in every possible way that it was a fascist country, that we were bloodsuckers, that we were annihilating our people, that our people were not with us, and so forth.

We must remind them, so that they may remember and have this in mind today when again they want to throw the blame for the events in Poland and Hungary on our shoulders. This perfidious tendency originates from those Stalinist elements which have succeeded in various parties in still maintaining their positions, and which would like again to strengthen their rule and to impose these

Stalinist tendencies upon their peoples and other peoples too. I will return to this later.

Now, I would like only to say to you that today we must consider the events in Hungary in the light of this entire development. At its own desire and initiative, we normalized our relations with the Soviet Union. When Stalin died, the new Soviet leaders saw that, thanks to Stalin's madness, the Soviet Union was brought into a very difficult situation. It found itself in a deadlock both in its foreign and domestic policies and, by its attitude of a dogmatic priest in forcing its own methods, in its relations with other people's democratic countries.

They realized where the main cause of all these difficulties lay, and at the Twentieth Congress they condemned Stalin's actions and his policies followed up to then, but they wrongly considered the whole thing as the question of the "cult of personality" and not as a question of the system. And the cult of personality is, in fact, the product of a system. They have not launched a struggle against that system, or, if they have, they have done it more in silence, saying that on the whole everything was good but that, in his late life, since he was old, Stalin began going a little mad and to make various mistakes.

From the very beginning, we said that here it was not merely the question of the cult of personality but, rather, the question of a system which made the creation of the cult of personality possible, that it was necessary to strike at the roots unceasingly and persistently—and this is most difficult.

Where are these roots? In the bureaucratic apparatus, in the methods of leadership and the so-called one-man rule, in the disregard for the role and tendencies of the working masses, in various Enver Hoxhas, Shehus and other leaders of certain Western and Eastern parties who are resisting the democratization and the decisions of the Twentieth Congress and who contributed a great deal toward strengthening Stalin's system and who are working today to bring it back to life and to power—here are the roots which must be corrected.

As far as we are concerned, we have considerably advanced in our relations with the Soviet Union. We have improved these relations and have concluded a whole series of economic arrangements which are very useful for us, which have been concluded under very favorable conditions, and so forth.

Furthermore, two declarations were also adopted, one in Belgrade and the other in Moscow. Both these declarations should, in fact, be significant not only in our mutual relations but also in relations between all socialist countries, but unfortunately they have not been understood in this way.

It was thought: "Well, since the Yugoslavs are so stubborn, we will respect and implement these declarations, but they do not affect the others because the situation there is, nevertheless, a little different from that in Yugoslavia. Yugoslavia is an organized and disciplined state. The Yugoslavs have proved their worth because they have succeeded in maintaining themselves even in the most difficult times and in not allowing a restoration of the capitalist system, and so forth. This means: They are something different from you in the Eastern countries where we brought you to power."

But this is wrong, because those same elements which provoked such a resistance of Yugoslavia in 1948 also live in these Eastern countries, in Poland, Hungary and in others, in some more and in some less.

When we were preparing the declaration on our party relations in Moscow, mainly on relations between the League of Yugoslav Communists and the C.P.S.U. the going was a little more difficult. We could not agree completely but, nevertheless, the declaration was issued which, in our opinion, is intended for a wider circle than Yugoslavia and the Soviet Union.

We warned that those tendencies which once provoked such strong resistance in Yugoslavia existed in all countries, and that one day they might find expression in other countries, too. Then it would be far more difficult to rectify this.

You know that Khrushchev was here for a rest. On that occasion, we had talks here and many more in Belgrade. As I and Comrades Rankovic and Pucar were invited to the Crimea, we went there and continued the talks. We saw that it would be rather difficult going for other countries. The Soviet leaders had a different attitude toward other countries. They had certain wrong

and defective views on relations with these countries—
with Poland, Hungary and others.

However, we did not take this too tragically, because
we saw that this was not the attitude of the entire Soviet
leadership, but only of a section which imposed this attitude upon the other to a certain extent. We saw that
this attitude was imposed rather by those people who
stood, and are still standing, on Stalinist positions, but
that there were still possibilities that, within the Soviet
leadership, those elements would win through internal
evolution which stand for stronger and more rapid development in the direction of democratization, abandonment of all Stalinist methods, the creation of new relations among socialist states, and development in this same
direction in foreign policy as well.

By certain indications, and also in conversations, we
saw that these elements were not weak, that they were
strong, but that this internal process of development in a
progressive direction—in the direction of abandoning
Stalinist methods—was also hindered by certain Western
countries which, by their propaganda and ceaseless repetition of the need for the liberation of these countries,
are interfering in their internal affairs and hindering a
rapid development and improvement in these countries.

The Soviet Union believes that, in view of the fact that
this interference in internal affairs has assumed rather
extensive proportions through propaganda disseminated
by radio broadcasts, the dispatch of materials by balloons,
and so forth, unpleasant consequences could result if it
left these countries completely and gave them, say, a
status such as that enjoyed by Yugoslavia. They are afraid
that reactionary forces might then be victorious in these
countries.

In other words, this means that they lack sufficient confidence in the internal revolutionary forces of these countries.

In my opinion, this is wrong. The origin of all later
mistakes lies in insufficient confidence in the socialist
forces of these people. When the Poznan affair [Polish
riots that began June 28, 1956] happened—you know
about it—the Soviet people suddenly changed their attitude toward us. They began getting colder. They thought
that we Yugoslavs were responsible.

Yes, we are responsible, because we live in this world, because we are what we are, because we created Yugoslavia as such, and because this Yugoslavia also acts outside its borders. Even if we did not want it so, our country acts, and very positively and usefully, at that.

Thanks to the fact that in Poland, despite all the persecutions and Stalinist methods of destroying cadres, a nucleus headed by Gomulka has nevertheless remained—the nucleus which at the Eighth Plenum knew how effectively to take things into its own hands, bravely to stamp a seal to the new course, that is, the course toward democratization and complete independence, but also for good relations with the Soviet Union, and to offer a determined resistance to interference in their internal affairs.

Thanks to this, reactionary forces in Poland could not find expression, although these forces certainly did exist and had hoped that they would be able to rise to the surface as a result of a clash between Communists. Thanks to a mature thinking and attitude by Soviet leaders, who stopped interfering in time, things have stabilized considerably in Poland at present, and are developing quite well.

I cannot say that this positive development in Poland, which is very similar to ours, has met with any joy in other countries of the alleged—so-called socialist camp. No, they criticize it secretly and among themselves, but also publicly to a certain extent. In these countries, Poland has not even found such a measure of support as it found among the Soviet leaders, who agreed to such an attitude.

Among these various leading men in certain countries of the so-called socialist camp, and also in certain Western Communist parties, Poland did not find understanding because Stalinist elements are still there.

For instance, when . . . Enver Hoxha, who knows only how to say "Marxism-Leninism" and not a word more, writes an article about Yugoslavia and Poland, . . . he resolutely condemns the tendencies of [a country's] own road and development according to specific conditions, and even goes against what Khrushchev and other Soviet leaders have recognized, that is, that there are specific roads to socialism.

Such a type not only dares slander and to stand up

against Yugoslavia and another great socialist country, but also hits the Soviet leaders themselves. Such Stalinist elements believe that people of the Stalinist cast will be found in the Soviet Union who will assist them maintain themselves on the backs of their people. This, comrades, is fatal. . . .

— 6 —

PRAVDA ASSAILS TITO FOR ATTACKING "STALINIST" FORCES*

November 23, 1956

. . . Among foreign reactions to the events in Hungary, Comrade Tito's recent speech in Pula attracts attention. It devotes a great deal of attention to the events in Hungary and correctly notes that the counterrevolutionary elements played a provocational role in them. . . .

The events in Hungary were the first large-scale sally of fascism in the entire postwar period, a sally which showed that the threat of fascism has not yet passed. Under these conditions, ideological solidarity, intense vigilance and deep adherence to principle in raising questions relating to the Hungarian events are required of all the supporters of socialism.

All the more astonishing, therefore, are certain propositions in Tito's speech which by no means contribute either to consolidation of all the supporters of socialism or to a correct understanding of a number of important problems of the international situation and of the current tasks of the world Communist movement.

To begin with, Tito's speech contains, along with correct evaluations of the Hungarian events, evaluations

* *Current Digest of the Soviet Press,* Vol. VIII, 1956. Reprinted by permission.

which cannot but evoke legitimate objections. "See," said Tito to his audience, "how strongly a people can resist, barehanded and badly armed, if they have before them one goal—to free themselves and to be independent. They are no longer interested in what sort of independence this would be or whether the bourgeoisie and the reactionary system would be restored in the country. Their only concern is to be independent as a nation. This is what was chiefly in their minds." In the first place, Comrade Tito obviously exaggerates when he speaks in this case of "the people." Secondly, Marxism-Leninism teaches us to examine such phenomena in a different way. If it is a matter of indifference to a section of the working people whether or not the yoke of exploitation is put on their necks (under the guise of false slogans of "freedom and independence"), whether or not their country is made a plaything in the hands of the big imperialist powers, whether or not they are plunged into a new war, as the fascist-Hitlerite clique of Horthy plunged the Hungarian people into a war in 1941-1944, this means that that section of the working people has fallen into the trap set by reaction. This would mean, consequently, that the masses are not moving toward liberation and independence but in a diametrically opposite direction, toward enslavement and loss of independence. Marxism-Leninism requires that in approaching social phenomena an answer always be given to the following direct question: which classes have an interest in the events in question; the interests of which class are served by a given form of public activity? It is true that considerable strata of the working people were drawn into the whirlpool of events in Hungary. History knows many instances in which the national feelings of the masses have been incited, inflamed and utilized by reactionary forces against the fundamental interests of the people. . . .

Speaking of the Hungarian events, Comrade Tito also makes a number of critical comments about the Communist Party of the Soviet Union. Special note should be made of these comments. We, of course, are not against criticism. The Moscow declaration states as the common opinion of the C.P.S.U. and the Yugoslav League of Communists that our cooperation will be based on friendly criticism and on a comradely exchange of opinions on contentious issues between our parties. We have no reason to retract this decision. But Comrade Tito's critical remarks arrest our attention because they were made in a tone that had almost disappeared in the recent period.

Let us take the main proposition advanced by Tito with regard to the Soviet system. He persistently emphasizes that the "cult of the individual leader was essentially the product of a specific system." He states that one must speak of the "system that gave rise to the creation of the cult of the individual." In reality, however, the cult of the individual was a flagrant contradiction of our entire Soviet socialist system. It was by proceeding from our political and economic system that we were able to wage a struggle against the cult of the individual and to achieve in a short period of time great successes in eliminating its consequences. . . .

How, then, can we interpret Tito's comments about our system other than as an attempt to cast a shadow on the Soviet people's system of social life? How can we fail to ask if this is not a repetition of previous attacks on the Soviet Union, which were fashionable in the past, when relations between the U.S.S.R. and Yugoslavia were deteriorating? It is for the Yugoslav people themselves and the Yugoslav League of Communists to decide what forms and methods they want to use in building socialism, but is it right to disparage the socialist system of other countries, to extol one's own experience, publicizing it as universal and the best? One cannot but see that the idea is appearing more and more often in the Yugoslav press that the "Yugoslav road to socialism" is the most correct or even the only possible road for almost all countries of the world. Furthermore, no mention is made of the favorable aspects and achievements of socialist construction in other countries. Such a position reminds one of the old proverb: "Without us even the sun cannot rise!"

*   *   *

The creative diversity on the single path of socialist development is determined in different countries by concrete, objective conditions.

The great Chinese People's Republic has gained outstanding experience in building socialism. Working in complex historical conditions, the Communist Party of China is making a tremendous contribution to the theory and practice of building a socialist society. The world communist movement can rightly be proud of the ability of the Chinese comrades to discover and successfully apply new methods of solving very complex problems in the life of hundreds of millions of people. However, the Chinese comrades constantly point out that they in no way claim that their methods have fully justified themselves in their country. The wisdom of the leadership of the Communist Party of China is also seen in the fact that it does not counterpose the experience of building socialism in its country to the experience of other countries, but skilfully uses the experience of all the socialist countries for the successful solution of problems in building a new society in China.

There is much that is unique in the solution of various problems of building socialism in the European people's democracies also. The experience of economic and cultural development in Poland, Rumania and Albania, the experience of forming agricultural cooperatives in Bulgaria and the substantial achievements in the development of industry and agriculture in Czechoslovakia—all this and much more enrich the treasury of experience in creating a new social system.

In Yugoslavia there are also unique forms of socialist construction. New methods and techniques of administration and economic management are being tested in practice. The workers' councils in Yugoslavia appeared comparatively recently. Every year of their existence brings correctives in their functions, but certain favorable aspects of this form are apparent even now. This cannot be said about another innovation, one which has had an adverse effect, namely, certain measures in the sphere of planning that have weakened the planned basis of the Yugoslav economy and increased the influence of market relations, a fact about which the Yugoslav press has also written.

There can be no doubt that good experience will always find adherents and followers if it has withstood the test of time and yielded positive results. Conversely, it is

ridiculous to take offense at other countries if one method
or another applied in one country is considered unsuitable
for another. . . .

In his speech Comrade Tito advances the slogan of
"independence" of the socialist countries and Communist
Parties from the Soviet Union and the Communist Party
of the Soviet Union. However, everyone knows that the
Soviet Union does not demand any dependence or subordination of anyone. This is stated with the utmost force
in the decisions of the 20th Party Congress. These principles are affirmed once again in the U.S.S.R. Government's Declaration of October 30, 1956, on the Principles
of Development and Further Strengthening of Friendship
and Cooperation between the Soviet Union and Other
Socialist States. Our party and our government are rec-
tifying past mistakes on this score with the utmost determination. This is borne out by the experience of our
relations with Yugoslavia in recent years. We acted
boldly to eradicate all past mistakes in our relations with
Yugoslavia, disregarding all considerations of prestige,
and we were the first to offer our hand to the Yugoslav
government and to the League of Communists. No one
can deny that for its part the Communist Party of the
Soviet Union has done and is doing everything necessary
to improve relations on the ideological basis of Marxism-
Leninism in the interests of strengthening friendship and
cooperation with the fraternal people of Yugoslavia and
in the interests of the struggle for peace and socialism.

While making a generally favorable evaluation of the
development of Soviet-Yugoslav relations and of the
agreements concluded between the U.S.S.R. and Yugoslavia, Tito rebukes the Soviet leaders for allegedly not
wishing to extend the principles set forth in these agreements to the other socialist countries. Tito needed this
strange and completely far-fetched assertion in order to
ascribe to the Soviet Union "insufficient trust" in the
socialist forces of the people's democracies.

These assertions are refuted by the facts. . . .

As is well known, the 20th Party Congress devoted
much attention to questions of the correct relations, based
on the fundamental positions of Marxism-Leninism, between our party and all the other fraternal Communist
and Workers' Parties. To speak now, after the 20th

Congress, about certain "Stalinists" in the C.P.S.U. who are supposedly trying to subordinate the fraternal parties means simply to close one's eyes to the policy which the C.P.S.U. is actually carrying out vis-à-vis the socialist countries. This policy is based on the principles of full equality, respect for territorial integrity, state independence and sovereignty and noninterference in one another's internal affairs and is imbued with the spirit of strengthening friendship among peoples and the spirit of proletarian socialist internationalism. This policy is imbued with concern for strengthening the friendship, fraternal cooperation and unity of all the countries in the socialist camp and concern for strengthening world peace.

What does Comrade Tito call for in his speech? To go it alone? But it may be asked: What does this path promise, what advantages does it hold for the socialist countries? There are no such advantages. The appeal to break with the other socialist states, with the entire fraternal family of socialist countries, cannot be of any benefit to the cause of building a socialist society. Loyalty to the great banner of socialist internationalism, solidarity and unity of all fighters for socialism—this is a major condition for the success of our great cause.

*   *   *

In the light of the requirements of socialist internationalism, one cannot but be surprised at the tone in which Comrade Tito found it possible to speak of the Communist Parties and their leaders. Without any grounds, he lists as "Stalinists" all the leading figures of the fraternal parties of the West and East who do not agree with his point of view, and he attributes the worst characteristics to them. He does not speak of them in any other way than as "inveterate Stalinist elements," "irresponsible elements in various Communist Parties," etc. The whole speech at Pula abounds in such attacks on Communist figures. Having chosen the question of mutual relations among the Communist Parties as the subject of his speech, Tito did not, in essence, hold a comradely discussion, did not debate, but tried to teach or, rather, abused various leaders of the Communist and Workers' Parties. The speech was not at all delivered in the tone of a conversation or debate on an equal basis, with proper respect for different opinions. Yet there are no grounds for speaking of "Stalinists" and "Stalinism," since our party, as well as the other Communist Parties, has defended and will defend the revolutionary principles of Marxism-Leninism.

Particularly inadmissible is the disdainful attitude in his speech toward such a country as Albania and toward its leaders. Speaking of the Albanian comrades, Tito used rude and insulting expressions. At the same time, it is well known that the Yugoslav leaders have frequently come out in defense of the thesis of the equality of large and small nations and of the right of each nation to have its own opinion and to defend it. Usually they insist that no one can claim a monopoly in defining truth. Yet hardly had Comrade Enver Hoxha written an article that displeased the Yugoslav comrades, then they hurled abuse at him. It is possible that the article could have been written differently. But why should Comrade Hoxha not have his opinion and that right to criticize which the Yugoslav comrades claim?

. . . After all that has been said, it is not surprising that Comrade Tito's speech has been met with rejoicing in bourgeois circles abroad. One cannot but recall here the words of the veteran of the workers' movement August Bebel, who recommended that one ponder one's behavior if one is praised by the enemy. Our enemies are now jumping to the conclusion that this speech will cause serious differences between the Soviet and Yugoslav Communists and will lead to a deterioration in Soviet-Yugoslav relations.

Who does not see that for the common cause of the Communist Parties it is inadmissible to inflame disputes, to indulge in mutual recriminations and to return to the atmosphere of differences which, through mutual efforts, have disappeared into the past? The highest interests of the cause of the working class and the interests of socialism persistently require the attainment of mutual understanding and the elimination of everything that is fraught with negative consequences for the further solidarity of the forces of socialism on the basis of Marxist-Leninist principles.

The Declaration on Relations Between the Yugoslav

League of Communists and the Communist Party of the Soviet Union points out that cooperation between the C.P.S.U. and the Yugoslav League of Communists must be based upon completely voluntary participation and equality, friendly criticism and comradely exchange of views on issues between our parties. It is well known that in the past incorrect views on certain important questions of socialist construction, views which do not accord with Marxist-Leninist theory, have been widespread among some figures in the Yugoslav League of Communists, and there have been deviations from the principles of proletarian internationalism. In moving toward a rapprochement with the Yugoslav League of Communists, our party bore in mind that the attainment of a unity of views on important ideological questions would require considerable time, since there were and still are differences on a number of problems of an ideological nature between the Communist Party of the Soviet Union and the Yugoslav League of Communists.

For its part, the C.P.S.U. will continue to conduct a policy of cooperation between our parties on a principled Marxist-Leninist basis in the interests of the fraternal peoples of the U.S.S.R. and Yugoslavia and in the interests of defending peace, democracy and socialism. We are convinced that today too disputed questions must be discussed and clarified in a calm, friendly atmosphere by means of a comradely exchange of views.

MORE ON HISTORICAL EXPERIENCE OF PROLETARIAN DICTATORSHIP

December 29, 1956*

. . . The publication in Chinese newspapers of Comrade Tito's speech of November 11, and the comments on that speech by various Communist Parties, has led people again to raise many questions which call for an answer.

. . . The attitude taken by Comrade Tito and other leading comrades of the Yugoslav League of Communists towards Stalin's mistakes and other related questions, as their recent views indicate, cannot be regarded by us as well-balanced or objective. It is understandable that the Yugoslav comrades bear a particular resentment against Stalin's mistakes. In the past, they made worthy efforts to stick to socialism under difficult conditions. Their experiments in the democratic management of economic enterprises and other socialist organizations have also attracted attention. The Chinese people welcome the reconciliation between the Soviet Union and other socialist countries on the one hand, and Yugoslavia on the other, as well as the establishment and development of friendly relations between China and Yugoslavia. Like the Yugoslav people, the Chinese people hope that Yugoslavia will become ever more prosperous and powerful as it advances to socialism. We also agree with some of the points in Comrade Tito's speech, for instance, his condemnation of the Hungarian counter-revolutionaries,

---

* Article prepared by the Editorial Department of the *Jen Min Jih Pao* (December 29, 1956) on the basis of a discussion at an enlarged meeting of the Political Bureau of the Central Committee of the Communist Party of China.

his support for the Worker-Peasant Revolutionary Government of Hungary, his condemnation of Britain, France and Israel for their aggression against Egypt, and his condemnation of the French Socialist Party for adopting a policy of aggression. But we are amazed that, in his speech, he attacked almost all the socialist countries and many of the Communist parties. Comrade Tito made assertions about "those hard-bitten Stalinist elements who in various parties have managed still to maintain themselves in their posts and who would again wish to consolidate their rule and impose those Stalinist tendencies upon their people, and even others." Therefore, he declared, "Together with the Polish comrades we shall have to fight such tendencies which crop up in various other parties, whether in the Eastern countries or in the West." We have not come across any statement put forward by leading comrades of the Polish United Workers Party, saying that it was necessary to adopt such a hostile attitude towards brother parties. We feel it necessary to say in connection with these views of Comrade Tito's that he took up a wrong attitude when he set up so-called "Stalinism," "Stalinist elements," etc. as objects of attack and maintained that the question now was whether the course "begun in Yugoslavia" or the so-called "Stalinist course" would win out. This can only lead to a split in the Communist movement.

Comrade Tito correctly pointed out that "viewing the current development in Hungary from the perspective—socialism or counter-revolution—we must defend Kadar's present government, we must help it." But help to and defense of the Hungarian Government can hardly be said to be the sense of the long speech on the Hungarian question made before the National Assembly of the Federal People's Republic of Yugoslavia by Comrade Kardelj, Vice-President of the Federation Executive Council of Yugoslavia. In the interpretation of the Hungarian incident he gave in his speech, Comrade Kardelj not only made no distinction whatsoever between ourselves and the enemy, but he told the Hungarian comrades that "a thorough change is necessary in the [Hungarian] political system." He also called on them to turn over state power wholly to the Budapest and other regional workers' councils, "no matter what the workers' councils have

become," and declared that they "need not waste their
efforts on trying to restore the Communist Party." "The
reason," he said, "was because to the masses the Party
was the personification of bureaucratic despotism." Such
is the blue-print of the "anti-Stalinist Course" which
Comrade Kardelj designed for other countries. The comrades in Hungary rejected this proposal of Comrade
Kardelj. They dissolved the Budapest and other regional
workers' councils which were being controlled by counter-revolutionaries and persisted in building up the socialist workers' party. We consider that the Hungarian
comrades are entirely right to act in this way, because
otherwise Hungary's future would belong not to socialism
but to counter-revolution.

Clearly, the Yugoslav comrades are going too far. Even
if some part of their criticism of brother parties is reasonable, the basic stand and method they adopt infringe
the principles of comradely discussion. We have no wish
to interfere in the internal affairs of Yugoslavia, but
the matters mentioned above are by no means internal.
In order to consolidate unity of the international Communist ranks and avoid creating conditions which the
enemy can use to cause confusion and division in our own
ranks, we cannot but offer our brotherly advice to the
Yugoslav comrades.

*　　　*　　　*

One of the grave consequences of Stalin's mistakes was
the growth of doctrinairism. While criticizing Stalin's
mistakes, the Communist parties of various countries
have waged a struggle against doctrinairism. This struggle is entirely necessary. But by adopting a negative attitude towards everything connected with Stalin, and by
putting up the erroneous slogan of "de-Stalinization,"
some Communists have helped to foster a revisionist
trend against Marxism-Leninism. This revisionist trend
is undoubtedly of help to the imperialist attacks against
the Communist movement, and the imperialists are in
fact making active use of it. While resolutely opposing
doctrinairism, we must at the same time resolutely oppose
revisionism.

Marxism-Leninism holds that there are common, basic
laws in the development of human society, but each state

and nation has features different from those of others. Thus all nations pass through the class struggle, and will eventually arrive at Communism, by roads that are the same in essence but different in their specific forms. The cause of the proletariat in a given country will triumph only if the universal truth of Marxism-Leninism is properly applied in the light of its special national features. And so long as this is done, the proletariat will accumulate new experience, thus making its contribution to the cause of other nations and to the general treasury of Marxism-Leninism. Doctrinaires do not understand that the universal truth of Marxism-Leninism manifests itself concretely and becomes operative in real life only through the medium of specific national characteristics. They are not willing to make a careful study of the social and historical features of their own countries and nations or to apply in a practical way the universal truth of Marxism-Leninism in the light of these features. Consequently they cannot lead the proletarian cause to victory.

Since Marxism-Leninism is the scientific summing up of the experience of the working class movement of various countries, it follows that it must attach importance to the question of applying the experience of advanced countries.

. . . But there must be a proper method of learning. All the experience of the Soviet Union, including its fundamental experience, is bound up with definite national characteristics, and no other country should copy it mechanically. Moreover, as has been pointed out above, part of Soviet experience is that derived from mistakes and failures. For those who know how best to learn from others this whole body of experience, both of success and failure, is an invaluable asset, because it can help them avoid roundabout ways in their progress and reduce their losses. On the other hand, indiscriminate and mechanical copying of experience that has been successful in the Soviet Union—let alone that which was unsuccessful there—may lead to failures in another country. . . .

Errors of doctrinairism, whenever and wherever they occur, must be set right. We shall continue our efforts to correct and prevent such errors in our work. But opposition to doctrinairism has nothing in common with

tolerance of revisionism. Marxism-Leninism recognizes
that the Communist movements of various countries
necessarily have their own national characteristics. But
this does not mean that they do not share certain basic
features in common, or that they can depart from the
universal truth of Marxism-Leninism. In the present anti-
doctrinaire tide, there are people in our country and
abroad who, on the pretext of opposing the mechanical
copying of Soviet experience, try to deny the international
significance of the fundamental experience of the Soviet
Union and, on the plea of creatively developing Marxism-
Leninism, try to deny the significance of the universal
truth of Marxism-Leninism.

Because Stalin and the former leaders in some socialist
countries committed the serious mistake of violating socialist democracy, some waverers in Communist ranks, on
the pretext of developing socialist democracy, attempt to
weaken or renounce the dictatorship of the proletariat,
the democratic centralism of the socialist state, and the
leading role of the Party. . . .

Among those who are trying to revise Marxism-
Leninism on the pretext of combating doctrinairism,
there are some who simply deny that there is a demarca-
tion line between the proletarian and the bourgeois dictatorships, between the socialist and the capitalist systems
and between the socialist and the imperialist camps. According to them, it is possible for certain bourgeois countries to build socialism without going through a proletarian revolution led by the Party of the proletariat and
without setting up a state led by the same, that state
capitalism in those countries is socialism itself, and
even human society as a whole has already been "growing
into" socialism. But while these people are publicizing
such ideas, the imperialists are mobilizing all available
military, economic, diplomatic, espionage and "moral"
forces, actively preparing to "undermine" and "disrupt"
socialist countries which have been established for many
years. . . .

In the interests of the common cause of the proletariat
of different countries, of joint resistance to the attack on
the socialist cause by the imperialist camp headed by the
United States, and of the economic and cultural upsurge
common to all socialist countries, we must continue to

strengthen international proletarian solidarity with the Soviet Union as its center.

International solidarity of the Communist parties is an entirely new type of relationship in human history. It is natural that its development cannot be free from difficulties. The Communist parties must seek unity with each other as well as maintain their respective independence. Historical experience proves that mistakes are bound to occur if there is no proper integration of these two aspects; if one or the other is neglected. Should the Communist parties maintain relations of equality among themselves and reach common understanding and take concerted action through genuine, and not nominal, exchange of views, their unity will be strengthened. Conversely, if, in their mutual relations, one party imposes its views upon others, or if the parties use the method of interference in each other's internal affairs instead of comradely suggestions and criticism, their unity will be impaired. . . .

To strengthen the international solidarity of the socialist countries, each Communist Party must respect the national interests and sentiments of other countries. This is of special importance for the Communist Party of a larger country in its relations with that of a small country. To avoid any resentment on the part of the small country, the Party of a larger country must constantly take care to maintain an attitude of equality. . . .

As we have already said, Stalin displayed certain greatnation chauvinist tendencies in relations with brother parties and countries. The essence of such tendencies lies in being unmindful of the independent and equal status of the Communist parties of various lands and that of the socialist countries within the framework of international bonds of union. There are definite historical reasons for such tendencies. The time-worn habits of big countries in their relations with small countries continue to make their influence felt in certain ways, while a series of victories achieved by a Party or a country in its revolutionary cause is apt to give rise to a certain sense of superiority.

For these reasons, systematic efforts are needed to overcome great-nation chauvinist tendencies. Great-Nation chauvinism is not peculiar to any one country. . . .

But it is not only great-nation chauvinism that hinders

international proletarian unity. In the course of history, big countries have shown disrespect for small countries and even oppressed them; and small countries have distrusted big ones and even become hostile to them. Both tendencies still exist to a greater or lesser extent among the peoples and even in the ranks of the working class of various countries. That is why, in order to strengthen the international solidarity of the proletariat, apart from the primary task of overcoming great-nation chauvinist tendencies in bigger countries, it is also necessary to overcome nationalist tendencies in smaller countries. . . .

Stalin's mistakes aroused grave dissatisfaction among people in certain East European countries. But then neither is the attitude of some people in these countries toward the Soviet Union justified. Bourgeois nationalists try their best to exaggerate the shortcomings of the Soviet Union and overlook the contributions it has made. They attempt to prevent the people from thinking how would the imperialists treat their country and their people if the Soviet Union did not exist. We Chinese Communists are very glad to see that the Communist parties of Poland and Hungary are already putting a firm check on the activities of evil elements that fabricate anti-Soviet rumors and stir up national antagonisms in relations with brother countries, and also that these parties have set to work to dispel nationalist prejudices existing among some sections of the masses and even among some of the Party members. This is clearly one of the steps urgently needed to consolidate friendly relations among the socialist countries. . . .

The Soviet Government's efforts to improve relations with Yugoslavia, its declaration of October 30, 1956, and its talks with Poland in November, 1956, all manifest the determination of the Communist Party of the Soviet Union and the Soviet Government to thoroughly eliminate past mistakes in foreign relations. These steps by the Soviet Union are an important contribution to the strengthening of the international solidarity of the proletariat. Obviously, at the present moment, when the imperialists are launching frenzied attacks on the Communist ranks in the various countries, it is necessary for the proletariat of all nations to strive to strengthen its solidarity. As we are faced with powerful enemies, no word or deed, no matter what name it goes by, which harms the solidarity of the international communist ranks, can hope to receive any sympathy from the Communists and working people of the various countries.

— 8 —

JOINT DECLARATION BY THE SOVIET UNION AND COMMUNIST CHINA

January, 1957*

. . . Both Government delegations note that in suppressing the national liberation movement and perpetrating aggression against the nations that have won their national independence, the aggressive imperialist alignments do not give up their attempts to conduct subversive activity against the Socialist states.

The armed uprising in Hungary was provoked by the imperialist aggressive quarters and the Hungarian counter-revolutionary elements, which made use of the dissatisfaction that the mistakes of the former leadership had caused among the Hungarian working people and youth.

They attempted to destroy the Socialist system in Hungary, to restore Fascist dictatorship and thereby create a hotbed of war in Europe.

By their conspiracy in Hungary, they tried to make a breach for the realization of their schemes of disuniting the Socialist states and smiting them one by one.

The swift defeat of the counter-revolutionary forces by the Hungarian people, led by the Hungarian Socialist Workers Party with the workers' and peasants' revolutionary government assisted by the Soviet Union, is a major victory of the cause of peace and socialism.

* New York *Times,* January 19, 1957. Reprinted by permission.

By helping the Hungarian people to put down the counter-revolutionary rebellion, the Soviet Union has fulfilled its duty to the working people of Hungary and the other Socialist states, which is completely in line with the interests of safeguarding world peace. . . .

The close unity and friendly cooperation of the Socialist countries is a reliable guarantee for the safeguarding of the cause of socialism and the strengthening of world peace.

In the present conditions, when imperialist aggressive circles step up their subversive and provocative activities against the Socialist countries, the further consolidation of the unity and cooperation between the Socialist countries becomes especially important.

The Socialist countries are united by the idea and cause of communism. Therefore, their mutual relations are based on the teaching of Marxism-Leninism, on the principles of proletarian internationalism. At the same time, the Socialist countries are independent and sovereign states, and relations between them are based also on the Leninist principles of national equality.

Such relations between Socialist countries represent a new type of international relations. These relations are subordinated to supreme interests—those of victory in the common cause of struggle against imperialism, of victory in the cause of building socialism in different countries, of victory in the common struggle for the triumph of communism.

Both parties believe that to strengthen and consolidate the unity of Socialist countries on the basis of the above principles is the supreme international duty of the Soviet Union and China.

The insidious plans of the imperialists to speculate on chauvinism, narrow nationalistic feelings and some survivals of national enmity in order to undermine and split the unity of the Socialist countries should in the final count be regarded as futile.

There are no essential contradictions and conflicting interests in the relations between the Socialist states. Even if in the past there were some mistakes and shortcomings in these relations, at the present time they are being overcome and eliminated. Moreover, these mistakes and shortcomings can by no means eclipse the fundamental and principal aspect in the relations between Socialist states—that of mutual assistance and cooperation.

Facts show that any questions of relations between the Socialist states can be fully solved on the basis of unity, through frank consultations and comradely discussion. It is fully possible to combine the unity of Socialist countries and the independence of each individual country in their relations.

Part III

The Readjustment of Policy: Unity, Diversity and the 1957 Congress of Communist Parties

The reverberations of the Hungarian and Polish revolts continued throughout 1957. Poland, and particularly Yugoslavia, resisted the gravitational pull of the center while professing to maintain correct fraternal relations with the other members of the Communist Bloc. Events in Communist China and in the Soviet Union—Mao's unhappy experience with internal decompression during the Hundred Flowers episode and Khrushchev's marginal victory over a hostile majority of the Politburo—exerted pressures to redefine and modify the policies of the Communist movement in line with the experiences gained in the period since the "turning point" of February 1956.

For a number of reasons a conference of Communist Parties in power appeared best suited to accomplish the purpose of the codification of doctrine. Old habits of conformity among most of the member states of the Socialist camp insured that the Soviet view would have majority support. Though Communist China could be expected to urge more doctrinaire views on the conference than would be palatable to the Soviet Party, her isolation in ideological questions and her dedication to the cause of communist unity could be counted on to prevail over particular ideological preferences, at the cost of minor theoretical concessions.

Also, the fact that 11 of the 13 governing Communist Parties were backing a Moscow-centered definition of Proletarian Internationalism was expected to force ideological compliance from the two intransigents, Poland

and Yugoslavia. Poland, indeed, submitted to the collective weight of the international assembly.

Tito, after studying a preliminary draft of the proposed Unity Declaration, did not personally attend the Moscow Conference. As a gesture of appeasement he postponed the 7th Congress of the CPY until 1958 and sent Kardelj and Rankovic to represent the Yugoslav Communist Party at the Moscow Meeting. Unable to modify the Unity Declaration, they did not sign it.

— 9 —

TEXT OF A JOINT COMMUNIQUE ON TALKS AMONG DELEGATES OF COMMUNIST AND WORKERS' PARTIES

Moscow, November 14-16, 1957*

DECLARATION
MEETING OF REPRESENTATIVES OF THE COMMUNIST AND WORKERS' PARTIES OF THE SOCIALIST COUNTRIES, HELD IN MOSCOW, NOV. 14 TO 16, 1957

Representatives of the Albanian Party of Labor, the Bulgarian Communist Party, the Hungarian Socialist Workers' Party, the Vietnamese Working People's Party, the Socialist Unity Party of Germany, the Communist Party of China, the Korean Party of Labor, the Mongolian People's Revolutionary Party, the Polish United Workers' Party, the Rumanian Workers' Party, the Communist Party of the Soviet Union and the Communist Party of Czechoslovakia discussed their relations, current problems of the international situation and the struggle for peace and socialism.

The exchange of opinions revealed identity of views of the parties on all the questions examined at the meeting and unanimity in their assessment of the international situation.

. . . The question of war or peaceful coexistence is

* New York *Times,* November 22, 1957. Reprinted by permission.

now the crucial question of world policy. All the nations must display the utmost vigilance in regard to the war danger created by imperialism.

At present the forces of peace have so grown that there is a real possibility of averting wars as was demonstrated by the collapse of the imperialist designs in Egypt. The imperialist plan to use the counter-revolutionary forces for the overthrow of the people's democratic system in Hungary has failed as well.

The cause of peace is upheld by the powerful forces of our era: the invincible camp of Socialist countries headed by the Soviet Union; the peace-loving countries of Asia and Africa taking an anti-imperialist stand and forming, together with the Socialist countries, a broad peace zone; the international working class and above all its vanguard, the Communist parties; the liberation movement of the peoples of the colonies and semi-colonies; the mass peace movement of the peoples; the peoples of the European countries who have proclaimed neutrality, the peoples of Latin America and the masses in the imperialist countries are putting up increasing resistance to the plans for a new war.

An alliance of these mighty forces could prevent war. but should the bellicose imperialist maniacs venture, regardless of anything, to unleash a war, imperialism will doom itself to destruction, for the peoples will not tolerate a system that brings them so much suffering and exacts so many sacrifices.

The Communist and workers' parties taking part in the meeting declare that the Leninist principle of peaceful coexistence of the two systems, which has been further developed and brought up to date in the decisions of the Twentieth Congress of the Soviet Communist party, is the sound basis of the foreign policy of the Socialist countries and the dependable pillar of peace and friendship among the peoples. The idea of peaceful coexistence coincides with the five principles advanced jointly by the Chinese People's Republic and the Republic of India and with the program adopted by the Bandung Conference of African-Asian countries. Peace and peaceful coexistence have now become the demands of the broad masses in all countries.

The Communist Parties regard the struggle for peace as

their foremost task. They will do all in their power to prevent war.

The meeting considers that in the present situation the strengthening of the unity and fraternal cooperation of the Socialist countries, the Communist and Workers' parties and the solidarity of the international working class, national liberation and democratic movements acquire special significance.

*   *   *

In the bedrock of the relations between the countries of the world Socialist system and all the Communist and workers' parties lie the principles of Marxism-Leninism, the principles of proletarian internationalism which have been tested by life. Today the vital interests of the working people of all countries call for their support of the Soviet Union and all the Socialist countries who, pursuing a policy of preserving peace throughout the world, are the mainstay of peace and social progress. The working class, the democratic forces and the working people everywhere are interested in tirelessly strengthening fraternal contacts for the sake of the common cause, in safeguarding from enemy encroachments the historic political and social gains effected in the Soviet Union—the first and mightiest Socialist power—in the Chinese People's Republic and in all the Socialist countries, in seeing these gains extended and consolidated.

The Socialist countries base their relations on principles of complete equality, respect for territorial integrity, state independence and sovereignty and non-interference in one another's affairs. These are vital principles. However, they do not exhaust the essence of relations between them. Fraternal mutual aid is part and parcel of these relations. This aid is a striking expression of Socialist internationalism. . . .

The Socialist countries are united in a single community by the fact that they are taking the common Socialist road, by the common class essence of the social and economic system and state authority, by the requirements of mutual aid and support, identity of interests and aims in the struggle against imperialism, for the victory of socialism and communism, by the ideology of Marxism-Leninism, which is common to all.

The solidarity and close unity of the Socialist countries constitute a reliable guarantee of the sovereignty and independence of each. Stronger fraternal relations and friendship between the Socialist countries call for a Marxist-Leninist internationalist policy on the part of the Communist and workers' parties, for educating all the working people in the spirit of combining internationalism with patriotism and for a determined effort to overcome the survivals of bourgeois nationalism and chauvinism. All issues pertaining to relations between the Socialist countries can be fully settled through comradely discussion, with strict observance of the principles of Socialist internationalism.

. . . The meeting confirmed the identity of views of the Communist and workers' parties on the cardinal problems of the Socialist revolution and Socialist construction. The experience of the Soviet Union and the other Socialist countries has fully borne out the correctness of the Marxist-Leninist proposition that the processes of the Socialist revolution and the building of socialism are governed by a number of basic laws applicable in all countries embarking on a socialist course. These laws manifest themselves everywhere, alongside a great variety of historic national peculiarities and traditions which must by all means be taken into account.

These laws are: Guidance of the working masses by the working class, the core of which is the Marxist-Leninist party, in effecting a proletarian revolution in one form or another and establishing one form or other of the dictatorship of the proletariat; the alliance of the working class and the bulk of the peasantry and other sections of the working people; the abolition of capitalist ownership and the establishment of public ownership of the basic means of production; gradual Socialist reconstruction of agriculture; planned development of the national economy aimed at building socialism and communism, at raising the standard of living of the working people; the carrying out of the Socialist revolution in the sphere of ideology and culture and the creation of a numerous intelligentsia devoted to the working class, the working people and the cause of socialism; the abolition of national oppression and the establishment of equality and fraternal friendship between the peoples; defense of the achievements of socialism against attacks by external and internal enemies; solidarity of the working class of the country in question with the working class of other countries, that is, proletarian internationalism.

Marxism-Leninism calls for a creative application of the general principles of the Socialist revolution and Socialist construction depending on the concrete conditions of each country, and rejects mechanical imitation of the policies and tactics of the Communist parties of other countries.

Lenin repeatedly called attention to the necessity of correctly applying the basic principles of communism, in keeping with the specific features of the nation, of the national state concerned. Disregard of national peculiarities by the proletarian party inevitably leads to its divorce from reality, from the masses and is bound to prejudice the cause of socialism. And, conversely, exaggeration of the role of these peculiarities or departure, under the pretext of national peculiarities, from the universal Marxist-Leninist truth on the Socialist revolution and Socialist construction is just as harmful to the Socialist cause.

The participants in the meeting consider that both these tendencies should be combated simultaneously. . . .

The theory of Marxism-Leninism derives from dialectical materialism. This world outlook reflects the universal law of development of nature, society and human thinking. It is valid for the past, the present and the future. . . . Of vital importance in the present stage is intensified struggle against opportunist trends in the working class and Communist movement. The meeting underlines the necessity of resolutely overcoming revisionism and dogmatism in the ranks of the Communist and workers' parties. Revisionism and dogmatism in the working class and Communist movement are today, as they have been in the past, international phenomena. Dogmatism and sectarianism hinder the development of Marxist-Leninist theory and its creative application in the changing conditions, replace the study of the concrete situation with merely quoting classics and sticking to books and lead to the isolation of the party from the masses. A party that has withdrawn into the shell of sectarianism and that has lost contact with the masses cannot bring victory to the cause of the working class.

In condemning dogmatism, the Communist parties believe that the main danger at present is revisionism or, in other words, right-wing opportunism, which as a manifestation of bourgeois ideology paralyzes the revolutionary energy of the working class and demands the preservation or restoration of capitalism. However, dogmatism and sectarianism can also be the main dangers at different phases of development in one party or another. It is for each Communist party to decide what danger threatens it more at a given time.

It should be pointed out that the conquest of power by the proletariat is only the beginning of the revolution, not its conclusion. After the conquest of power, the working class is faced with the serious tasks of effecting the Socialist reconstruction of the national economy and laying the economic and technical foundation of socialism. At the same time the overthrown bourgeoisie always endeavors to make a comeback, the influence exerted on society by the bourgeoisie, the petty bourgeoisie and their intelligentsia, is still great. That is why a fairly long time is needed to resolve the issue of who will win—capitalism or socialism. The existence of bourgeois influence is an internal source of revisionism, while surrender to imperialist pressure is its external source.

Modern revisionism seeks to smear the great teachings of Marxism-Leninism, declares that it is "outmoded" and alleges that it has lost its significance for social progress. The revisionists try to exorcise the revolutionary spirit of Marxism, to undermine faith in socialism among the working class and the working people in general. They deny the historical necessity for a proletarian revolution and the dictatorship of the proletariat during the period of transition from capitalism to socialism, deny the leading role of the Marxist-Leninist party, reject the principles of proletarian internationalism and call for rejection of the Leninist principles of party organization and, above all, of democratic centralism, for transforming the Communist party from a militant revolutionary organization into some kind of debating society.

The experience of the international Communist movement shows that resolute defense by the Communist and workers' parties of the Marxist-Leninist unity of their ranks and the banning of factions and groups sapping unity guarantee the successful solution of the tasks of the socialist revolution, the establishment of socialism and communism. . . .

The forms of the transition of socialism may vary for different countries. The working class and its vanguard—the Marxist-Leninist party—seek to achieve the Socialist revolution by peaceful means. This would accord with the interests of the working class and the people as a whole as well as with the national interests of the country.

Today in a number of capitalist countries the working class headed by its vanguard has the opportunity, given a united working-class and popular front or other workable forms of agreement and political cooperation between the different parties and public organizations to unite a majority of the people, to win state power without civil war and insure the transfer of the basic means of production to the hands of the people, relying on the majority of the people and decisively rebuffing the opportunist elements incapable of relinquishing the policy of compromise with the capitalists and landlords. The working class can defeat the reactionary, anti-popular forces, secure a firm majority in parliament, transform parliament from an instrument serving the class interests of the bourgeoisie into an instrument serving the working people, launch a non-parliamentary mass struggle, smash the resistance of the reactionary forces and create the necessary conditions for peaceful realization of the Socialist revolution.

All this will be possible only by broad and ceaseless development of the class struggle of the workers, peasant masses and the urban middle strata against big monopoly capital, against reaction, for profound social reforms, for peace and socialism.

In the event of the ruling classes' resorting to violence against people, the possibility of non-peaceful transition to socialism should be borne in mind. Leninism teaches, and experience confirms, that the ruling classes never relinquish power voluntarily. In this case the degree of bitterness and the forms of the class struggle will depend not so much on the proletariat as on the resistance put up by the reactionary circles to the will of the overwhelming majority of the people, on these circles using force at one or another stage of the struggle for socialism.

The possibility of one or another way to socialism depends on the concrete conditions in each country. . . .

After exchanging views, the participants in the meeting arrived at the conclusion that in present conditions it is expedient, besides bilateral meetings of leading personnel and exchange of information, to hold, as the need arises, more representative conferences of Communist and workers' parties to discuss current problems, share experience, study each other's views and attitudes and concert action in the joint struggle for the common goals—peace, democracy and socialism.

Part IV

The Struggle with Right-Wing Revisionism

Failure of the Yugoslavs to subscribe to the Unity Declaration worked out by the Communist World Movement in November, 1957, exposed the lone dissenter to the critical attack of the other Communist Parties. Initially, some hope remained for compromise. In March 1958, Yugoslavia circulated a preliminary draft of its Party Program among the members of the Communist bloc. Though it is only possible to speculate on the nature of the changes that Chinese and Soviet critics suggested, a comparison between early drafts and the final version of the Yugoslav Program would indicate that fraternal comments were largely ignored by the Yugoslav party leadership.

After the adoption of the program in April 1958, the nature of the debate between the three independent centers of Communism followed a set pattern. In the Soviet catalogue of Yugoslav sins, Yugoslavia's obdurate refusal to remain within the Socialist camp became the issue of primary concern. The obvious revisionist deviations of those sections of the program dealing with the domestic features of Yugoslavian socialism were of much less significance to the Soviets than to the Chinese. Peking, in a bitterly critical review of Belgrade's program and conduct, maintained consistently that the deficiencies of Yugoslavia's conduct toward the Socialist camp were caused directly by Tito's deliberate rejection of Marxism-Leninism and his espousal of Neo-Bernsteinist doctrines.

Ultimately, Peking and Moscow revived as "basically correct" the anti-Yugoslav Cominform resolution of 1948, which both had repudiated during 1955-1956.

In response to this bi-lateral effort to discredit the Yu-

goslav heresy, Tito's defensive arguments emphasized in essence the following two themes: (1) For Yugoslavia to join the Communist camp would aggravate the world situation by furthering the undesirable tendency of Capitalism and Socialism to divide the world into hostile blocs; (2) Furthermore, the bloc policies of Moscow and Peking would delay the extension of the Socialist system to other areas of the world, an effort for which the Yugoslavs apparently thought themselves and their program uniquely suited.

— 10 —

YUGOSLAVIA'S WAY— THE PROGRAM OF THE YUGOSLAV LEAGUE OF COMMUNISTS, 1958*

ON BILATERAL AND MULTILATERAL COOPERATION

The Yugoslav Communists do not make an issue of the form of cooperation among the Communist parties or between these parties and the Socialist or other progressive movements. They make a point of its content. They favor both bilateral and multilateral cooperation, provided it is always based on full equality, with no imposition of attitudes and no interference in the internal relations of the parties, and provided it serves the concrete interests of peace, socialism and social progress in general. The League of the Communists of Yugoslavia believes that both forms of cooperation are indispensable elements in uniting the actions of the socialist forces and the progressive efforts of humanity. If, however, the Yugoslav Communists under present conditions assign primary importance to the various forms of bilateral cooperation, they do so first because of the altered objective conditions of the contemporary development of socialism; and, second, because the earlier forms of multilateral cooperation of the workers' parties—aside from

* Translated by Stoyan Pribechevich. Copyright 1958, by All Nations Press, New York. Reprinted by permission.

their positive aspects whenever they corresponded to the given historic period—produced negative phenomena which caused considerable harm to the struggle for socialism and peace and which the labor movement must live down so that they may not again sully the democratic principles of socialist internationalism.

IDEOLOGICAL MONOPOLISM

Among these phenomena one must first mention tendencies toward ideological monopoly.

Tendencies toward ideological monopoly have always been a barrier to the development of socialist thinking and a source of dogmatism and opportunist-revisionist reaction. These tendencies gave rise to aspirations toward unconditional leadership in the labor movement, which led to many negative consequences at a time when not one single working class party was in power. Tendencies toward ideological monopoly can cause even greater damage after the parties of the working class have assumed power. It is the task of the labor movement—especially of the Communists of the larger, stronger, socialist countries, with greater responsibilities—to fight both in theory and in practice for an equality of relations, on the principle that the correctness and progressive character of an ideology or of certain forms of socialist construction depend exclusively on their vitality and verification by practice, not on the approval by some international forum.

Every aspect of ideological monopoly that hampers free socialist development in socialist countries is a brake on international socialism in general. For this reason, the League of the Communists of Yugoslavia regards as particularly useful today the creation of such forms of international cooperation as would on the broadest possible basis unite efforts toward solution of the common practical problems of peace and of the struggle for, and the building of, socialism.

The interest of further socialist development demands free, socialist, democratic relations among the parties of the socialist countries. In the struggle for the victory of socialism, the working class of one country or another may for a certain period of time be the standard-bearer, may stand in the front ranks or have a superior material force at its disposal. But this does not mean that it thus acquires a monopoly position in the labor movement, least of all in ideology. Past experience has shown—and it is even clearer today—that cooperation in the labor movement is possible only among equals.

Also characteristic of contemporary development is the fact that in several countries Communist parties have come to power. Thus, the question of relations among the Communist parties assumes yet another, historically new, aspect.

The leadership of Communist parties in power is responsible for the work of these parties not only to its membership but to the entire people. This fact must be reflected in the character of their mutual relations.

In their mutual relations, the Communist parties in power cannot make decisions belonging to the jurisdiction of representative organs elected by all citizens. The Communist parties in the practice of their international relations have so far often failed to keep this in mind, thus restricting the importance and role of the abovementioned representative organs.

To proclaim the path and form of the socialist development of any country as the only correct ones is nothing but dogma, obstructing the process of the socialist transformation of the world. The general aims of socialism are common, but the tempo and forms of the movement of society toward these aims are and must be different, depending on the concrete conditions in individual countries or parts of the world. Consequently, freedom of internal socialist development and absence of any imposition of various forms, non-interference in the internal life and progress of various movements, and a free and equal exchange of experience and socialist theoretical thought should be the basic principle of mutual relations among socialist countries and socialist movements.

Attempts at designating the admission of the diversity in forms of development of socialist processes as a "new" ideological phenomenon, as "national communism," have nothing in common with a scientific explanation of contemporary socialist development. Such theories can arise only in the minds of dogmatists, or are deliberately injected by the spokesmen of the bourgeoisie in order to introduce disorientation and ideological confusion into the labor movement. Such designs must not prevent the comprehension and working out of specific developments and the orientation of the working class primarily according to the problems and conditions of its own country. . . .

THE HISTORIC MEANING OF THE STRUGGLE FOR NATIONAL INDEPENDENCE

. . . In fighting for the independence of our country, the League of the Communists of Yugoslavia does not think of independence as seclusion or isolation.

The conflict which broke out in 1948 because of the resistance of the Communist Party of Yugoslavia to Stalin's policies did not express any desire on the part of the Yugoslav Communists to isolate themselves. It represented their resistance to improper hegemonist policies and practices which, once established, would have done enormous damage to the development of socialism. The resolutions of the Information Bureau of the Communist Parties (*Cominform*) attempted to legalize inequality among socialist countries. They were a negation of the independence of peoples and their freedom in developing socialist relations as a basis for rapprochement among peoples on their path to socialism.

All that happened in 1948 was a gross violation of socialist and democratic principles which ought to be observed in relations between two socialist countries. The lessons of the past years have shown that the development of relations among socialist countries should serve as an example and point to the need of creating better, more lasting and more comprehensive relations among nations. These relations must be based on the principles of independence, full equality and respect for the individuality of each separate country.

Resistance to improper practices in relations among socialist countries—resistance which in various ways has taken place more than once—has revealed the progressive aspirations of the peoples of the socialist countries: to build socialism in accordance with their specific conditions, having in mind the interests of socialism as a whole. To label this policy "national communism" can only be the result of dogmatic or great-power conceptions or of bourgeois ideological influence and intrigue.

The League of the Communists of Yugoslavia believes that relations among socialist countries must be cleansed of the negative traits which capitalism has introduced into the relations between the big and the small, the strong and the weak, the advanced and the backward, the white and the colored, the culturally developed and the culturally underdeveloped countries and peoples. . . .

THE PROBLEMS OF THE STRUGGLE FOR PEACE

. . . Peace in contemporary conditions primarily means peaceful coexistence of peoples and states with different social systems. This coexistence must not be passive, entrenched in bloc positions. It must be active, aiming at a constant widening of cooperation among peoples.

Active coexistence must, above all, mean creation of conditions necessary for a gradual resolution of controversial international issues: for disarmament; for release of enormous resources spent on armaments to raise, instead, the economic and cultural standards of the world; for aid to underdeveloped countries; for constructive, peaceful competition in economy, culture, science and other fields among countries with different social systems; and for developing the productive forces of society to a still higher degree through the utilization of all the latest achievements of science and technology.

In accordance with all this, the League of the Communists of Yugoslavia believes that an all-out effort is needed to overcome the existing division into blocs which renders cooperation among peoples difficult in every field of social life.

The realism of the policy of peace aiming at the elimination of the division of the world into blocs is based on the knowledge that differences in social and economic systems need not necessarily result in the formation of blocs, despite the fact that forces interested in such a division do exist in the world today. A large part of the world's population and territory stands outside the bloc alignments. Socialist Yugoslavia sees in the independent, non-bloc policies of these countries a contribution to the broadest international cooperation and to the consolidation of peace in the world. Although the policies of the uncommitted countries are not identical, although there are differences in their relations with the power blocs, they are all interested in finding a way out of the present situation by a comprehensive development of cooperation among all countries regardless of their social systems.

The social-economic and political meaning and roles of the existing blocs are different. The League of the Communists of Yugoslavia believes that the Warsaw Pact and similar measures of the socialist countries are a natural defense reaction to the creation of the Atlantic Pact and especially to the arming of Germany and the creation of military bloc organizations in Western Europe. Besides, in the last few years the Socialist countries have made a number of steps and proposals toward relaxation of international tensions and thus toward elimination of bloc barriers among nations. However, an effort in this direction is needed on the part of all peoples and all political factors having the interests of peace at heart. The League of the Communists of Yugoslavia will strive to have socialist Yugoslavia, which stands outside the military and political blocs, continue her contribution toward this end.

ACTIVE COEXISTENCE

The policy of active coexistence should rest on respect of independence, sovereignty, equality, territorial integrity, and non-interference in the internal affairs of other countries. Active coexistence can be established only in relations among individual states and peoples and not in relations between blocs of countries. There can be no coexistence between blocks. This would not be coexistence but a temporary truce concealing the danger of new conflicts.

The policy of active coexistence is both the expression and the need of the powerful development of productive forces. This development has brought about a factual interconnection of the whole world and a close interdependence of the economies of various countries. And it has made war senseless as a means of solving whatever problems and antagonisms exist among countries, in view of the inevitable catastrophe for mankind through the use of nuclear weapons. . . .

The policy of active coexistence inevitably leads in every capitalist country to the checking and weakening of the forces which act as brakes on progress and which, at the same time, harbor the potential danger of provoking a new world war. This policy broadens the basis of the struggle against imperialism and colonialism; reduces the possibilities of hegemonist policies; breaks up the foundation of bureaucratism, and facilitates a more rapid and less painful development of socialist countries. Consequently, far from perpetuating the existing social forms, this policy helps hasten their change. . . .

TASKS OF THE FOREIGN POLICY OF SOCIALIST YUGOSLAVIA

. . . In its foreign policy, by advocating active co-existence and removal of the rift caused by blocs, our country will continue to develop all possible activities through the United Nations and to struggle for its universality, thus contributing to the accomplishment of the purpose for which this organization was founded. Without underestimating the negative effects of the international situation on this organization or its frequently one-sided attitudes resulting from this situation, the League of the Communists of Yugoslavia believes that, through persistent efforts on the part of the democratic and anti-imperialist forces of peace, this organization could become, more than it has been, the common instrument of the strivings of the peoples for peace and for their rapprochement, cooperation and peaceful mutual assistance and aid.

EDITORIAL FROM THE *JEN MIN JIH PAO* (PEOPLE'S DAILY), PEIPING

May, 1958*

. . . The recently closed seventh congress of the League of Communists of Yugoslavia adopted a "Draft Program of the League of Communists of Yugoslavia" which is an anti-Marxist-Leninist, out-and-out revisionist program. . . .

The draft program openly forsakes the fundamental principles of Marxism-Leninism, sets itself against the declaration of the meeting of representatives of the Communist and workers' parties of Socialist countries held in Moscow last November, and at the same time repudiates the "Peace Manifesto" adopted by the meeting of representatives of sixty-four Communist and workers' parties, endorsed by the representatives of the League of Communists of Yugoslavia itself. The draft program brands all the basic principles of revolutionary theory established by Marx and Engels and developed by Lenin and other great Marxists as "dogmatism," and the leaders of the League of Communists of Yugoslavia style themselves "irreconcilable enemies of any dogmatism."

What are the most basic things in the "dogmatism" which the leaders of the League of Communists of Yugoslavia have chosen to attack? They are proletarian revolution and proletarian dictatorship. But it is common knowledge that without proletarian revolution and proletarian dictatorship there can be no socialism. The draft program of the League of Communists of Yugoslavia concentrates its opposition on proletarian revolution and its attack on proletarian dictatorship, smears the Socialist state and the Socialist camp and beatifies capitalism, the imperialist state and the imperialist camp. This cannot but give rise to doubt about the "socialism" avowed by

* New York *Times,* May 11, 1958. Reprinted by permission.

the leaders of the League of Communists of Yugoslavia.

Speaking like the reactionaries of all countries and the Chinese bourgeois Rightists, the leading group of the League of Communists of Yugoslavia has viciously slandered proletarian dictatorship, alleging that it "leads to bureaucratism, the ideology of statism, separation of the leading political forces from the working masses, stagnation, the deformation of Socialist development, and the sharpening of internal differences and contradictions." They maliciously slander the Socialist camp, alleging that it also has a policy of "positions of strength and struggle for hegemony." They describe the two radically different world politic-economic systems, the Socialist camp and the imperialist camp, as "division of the world into two antagonistic military-political blocs." They represent themselves as standing outside the "two blocs" of socialism and imperialism, or in a position beyond the blocs.

They hold that the U.S.-dominated United Nations can "bring about greater and greater unification of the world," that economic cooperation of all countries of the world, including the imperialist countries, is "an integral part of the Socialist road to the development of world economy." They maintain that "the swelling flow of state-capitalist tendencies in the capitalist world is the most tangible proof that mankind is irrepressibly and by the most diverse roads deeply entering into the epoch of socialism."

These propositions cannot but call to mind the revisionist preaching about "evolutionary socialism," "ultra-imperialism," "organized capitalism" and "the peaceful growing of capitalism into socialism" made by right-wing Socialists in the late nineteenth century and early twentieth century, such as Bernstein, Kautsky, Hilferding and their ilk, which were intended to induce the working class in the various capitalist countries to give up revolutionary struggle for socialism and uphold bourgeois rule. . . .

It is quite obvious that open and uncompromising criticism must be waged against the series of anti-Marxist-Leninist and out-and-out revisionist views assembled in the draft program of the League of Communists of Yugoslavia.

If theoretical criticism of the revisionism of Bernstein

and Kautsky and their ilk by the Marxists of the late nineteenth and early twentieth centuries was inevitable, then it is even more necessary now for us to criticize neo-Bersteinism.

This is because modern revisionism is propounded as a comprehensive and systematic program by the leading group of a party that wields state power. It is also because modern revisionism is aimed at splitting the international Communist movement and undermining the solidarity of the Socialist countries, and is directly detrimental to the fundamental interests of the Yugoslav people.

We consider as basically correct the criticism made in June, 1948, by the Information Bureau of Communist Parties in its resolution "Concerning the Situation in the Communist Party of Yugoslavia" in regard to the mistake of the Yugoslav Communist party in departing from the principles of Marxism-Leninism and sinking into bourgeois nationalism; but there were defects and mistakes in the method adopted at that time by the Information Bureau in dealing with this question. The resolution concerning Yugoslavia adopted by the Information Bureau in November, 1949, was incorrect and it was later withdrawn by the Communist and Workers' Parties which took part in the Information Bureau meeting.

Since 1954, the Soviet Union and other countries of the Socialist camp have done their utmost and taken various measures to improve their relations with Yugoslavia. This has been fully correct and necessary. The Communist parties of various countries have adopted an attitude of waiting patiently, hoping that the leaders of the League of Communists of Yugoslavia would return to the Marxist-Leninist standpoint in the interest of adherence by the Yugoslav people to the road of socialism.

However, the leading group of the League of Communists of Yugoslavia has spurned the well-intentioned efforts made by the Central Committee of the Communist Party of the Soviet Union and the Communists of other countries. Around the time of the Hungarian event, they tried to disrupt the unity of countries in the Socialist camp on the pretext of so-called "opposition to Stalinism"; during the Hungarian event, they supported the renegade Nagy clique; and, in their recent congress, they have gone further and put forward a systematic and comprehensive revisionist program.

The leaders of the League of Communists of Yugoslavia should think soberly: Will the League of Communists of Yugoslavia be able to maintain its solidarity with the Communist parties of other countries by abandoning the fundamental viewpoints of Marxism-Leninism and persisting in revisionist viewpoints? Can there be a basis for solidarity without a common Marxist-Leninist viewpoint? Will it be in the interests of the Yugoslav people to reject friendship with the countries in the Socialist camp and with the Communist parties of other countries?

— 12 —

ON "REVISIONISM": EXCERPTS FROM ARTICLES IN *KOMMUNIST*, OFFICIAL PUBLICATION OF THE YUGOSLAV COMMUNIST PARTY, May, 1958*

The authors of the (Chinese) article, in the name of Socialist Internationalism, proclaim the policy of a Socialist country as the Enemy No. 1.

They simply took the Cominform resolution of 1948 out of the archives, thrusting themselves on the League of Communists of Yugoslavia with all kinds of labels of various revisionist directions which appeared in definite historical conditions in different countries, and even with insinuations on serving the imperialists.

* New York *Times,* May 11, 1958. Reprinted by permission.

Taking over the logics and methods of the Cominform, the Chinese Communists set as their main task interference in Yugoslavia's internal affairs, struggle against Socialist Yugoslavia, the great struggle on which the success or failure of the cause of the working class in the world and the cause of socialism depend.

Ten years ago the authors of the first Cominform resolution also set themselves this same task. Perhaps it is useful to mention that, while setting as their chief task the struggle against Socialist Yugoslavia, and not the concern for their own people, for socialism in their own country and its proper development, the authors of the first resolution experienced an inglorious end, while Socialist Yugoslavia remained Socialist, firmer, stronger, more united than ever before.

What happened to most of those who signed the first Cominform resolution, which the Chinese comrades are now rehabilitating so lightly?

Out of seventeen signatories of the resolution from Socialist countries, twelve of them have finished ingloriously or tragically. Trajko Kostov was sentenced to death. Vulko Chervenkov was removed from the post of Prime Minister and sharply criticized. Ana Pauker was expelled from the party. Vasili Kuka was sentenced to life imprisonment. Matyas Rakosi led Hungary to the brink of ruin and now lives as an emigre away from his country. Mihaly Farkas is in prison for crimes against his fellow Communists. Erno Gero is also living as an emigre. Jakub Berman has been stigmatized in Poland for a breach of the law, for arresting and persecuting honest Communists. Georgi Maksimilianovich Malenkov has been condemned by the party for belonging to the well-known anti-party group. Gustav Bares has been removed from party functions. Rudolf Slansky was hanged. Bedzih Geminder was also hanged.

This tragic chapter from the past of the Socialist countries we are not mentioning because we consider it necessary to accuse anybody today, but in order to point to the paradoxical situation in which the authors of the article in Jenmin Jihpao have landed by fishing out of the archives the documents which the events have so tragically and mercilessly disproved.

Therefore, those who try to resuscitate the methods

which history has branded with condemnation take upon themselves a great responsibility.

Yugoslavia's attitude in individual questions has always been clearly and publicly expressed and in good time, so that its visualization did not call for any special patience. However, if some people think that friendly cooperation between Yugoslavia and other Socialist countries can develop only if the League of Communists changes its attitudes of principle, then the question arises: What ensures any equality of cooperation and where then do the methods and actions introduced by the article in Jenmin Jihpao differ from actions and methods declared in the first and second resolutions of the Cominform?

If this is the price and condition for cooperation, then what is involved is a problem exactly ten years old, and for Yugoslav Communists this price is unacceptable today just as it was ten years ago. And precisely in this lies, it seems, the meaning of the call to the leaders of the League of Communists of Yugoslavia to "ponder soberly" as to "whether it will be in the interests of the Yugoslav people to reject the friendship with the countries of the Socialist camp and with the Communist parties of other countries."

Striving always and resolutely—despite the campaign conducted against our country—for friendly relations and cooperation with all Socialist countries and Communist parties, and accepting on that line their initiative for normalization of relations, the Yugoslav Communists considered that the restoration of those relations means a break with the old harmful methods, which found their expression in the Cominform resolution, and the establishment of the only possible and normal practice in the relations between Socialist countries and Communist parties, which consists in that they develop their relations in the spirit of solidarity and friendship even when they differ in certain concrete aspects of the internal and international policy.

Nobody has the right to prescribe how the relations between Socialist countries should be, but every Socialist country is obliged to strive for the greatest possible cooperation within the framework of the common and equal interests of the Socialist countries. We have always endeavored to do this, even when we did not agree with certain attitudes of other Socialist countries and Communist parties. We also said that we did not agree with and refused to take part in actions with which we did not agree, but apart from this, we endeavored to co-operate in those fields where common attitudes and views existed and exist.

Those were precisely the essential questions of social-ism, that is, the questions of the struggle for peace, the questions of the struggle for the defense of socialism and Socialist system from every attempt of imperialist inter-ference from outside, the questions of cooperation in the struggle for strengthening all forces of social progress and socialism, as well as in the support to anti-imperialist forces in the struggle for national independence.

Of course, in the realization of these aims also, every country or Communist party should approach in keeping with the specific conditions in which it operates.

However, Jenmin Jihpao's article now sets matters dif-ferent. It does not only represent a reinforcement of the Cominform resolution against Yugoslavia, but also the establishment of the methods and actions which accom-panied the work of the Cominform and which marked a period which even its most conservative defenders today mark as a period in which a number of major "mistakes" were made.

If this is really the intention of the author of the arti-cle in Jenmin Jihpao, then not only cooperation between Yugoslavia and other Socialist countries and Communist parties will suffer from this, but the international social-ism generally as well.

EXCERPTS FROM KHRUSHCHEV'S SPEECH TO THE 21ST PARTY CONGRESS

January, 1959*

The conferences of representatives of Communist and Workers' Parties in November, 1957, demonstrated the complete unity of views of the fraternal parties. The conference declaration was unanimously approved by all the Communist and Workers' Parties and became a charter of international unity of the world Communist movement. The declaration condemned revisionism as the principal danger and also dogmatism and sectarianism. Life fully proved the declaration's conclusions to have been correct. And we are guided by them now. . . .

The international Communist movement has condemned the outlook and policies of the Yugoslav revisionists. The leaders of the League of Communists of Yugoslavia try to present matters as though the Marxist-Leninist parties had begun an ideological struggle against them because they refused to sign the declaration. This claim is utterly false. It was the Yugoslav leaders who countered the declaration by coming forth with their revisionist program, in which they attacked the Marxist-Leninist stand of the international Communist movement. One asks: Could Marxists have ignored these facts? Of course not. Therefore all parties that take Marxist-Leninist positions came forth with principled criticism of the program of the League of Communists of Yugoslavia.

Our position on the views of the Yugoslav leaders is clear. We have set it forth repeatedly in all frankness. But the Yugoslav leaders twist and turn, falsify, and dodge the truth.

* Current Digest of the Soviet Press, Vol. XI, Nos. 4 and 5. Reprinted by permission.

The Yugoslav leaders try to conceal the essence of their differences with the Marxist-Leninists. This is that the Yugoslav revisionists deny the necessity of international class solidarity and abandon working-class positions. They try to convince all and sundry that there are two blocs, two military camps, in the world. Yet everyone knows that the socialist camp, embracing the socialist countries of Europe and Asia, is not a military camp, but a community of equal peoples in the struggle for peace and for a better life for the working people, for socialism and communism. The other camp is the camp of the imperialists, seeking at any price to preserve the system of oppression and violence, and confronting mankind with the menace of war. We did not imagine these camps; they took shape in the course of social development.

The Yugoslav leaders claim that they stand aside from blocs and above the camps, although in actuality they belong to the Balkan bloc, consisting of Yugoslavia, Turkey and Greece. The latter two countries, as is known, are members of the aggressive NATO bloc, while Turkey belongs, moreover, to the Baghdad Pact. The leaders of the League of Communists of Yugoslavia greatly resent our telling them that they are sitting on two stools. They claim that they are seated on their own, the Yugoslav stool. But for some reason this Yugoslav stool is greatly supported by the American monopolies! And this position "outside of blocs," this neutrality that the leaders of the League of Communists of Yugoslavia advertise so much, carries a distinct odor of the American monopolies, which nourish "Yugoslav socialism." The history of class struggle contains no instance of the bourgeoisie materially or morally encouraging its class enemy and helping to build socialism. . . .

If Yugoslavia lags in her development, if she does not walk but staggers along the socialist path, the responsibility lies entirely on the revisionist, anti-Marxist line of the Yugoslav League of Communist leadership, which has its own particular view of the role of the party in building socialism. The Yugoslav revisionists minimize the Party's role and in effect reject the Leninist doctrine that the Party is the guiding force in the struggle for socialism. . . .

We have the very friendliest feelings for the fraternal peoples of Yugoslavia, for the Yugoslav Communists, heroes of underground and partisan struggle. On many questions of foreign policy we speak a common language. We shall continue to develop trade with Yugoslavia on a reciprocal basis. We shall seek to cooperate with Yugoslavia on all the questions of the anti-imperialist and peace struggle on which our attitudes shall coincide.

How will matters stand in the Party sphere? Everything will depend on the League of Communists of Yugoslavia. Its leaders have themselves isolated themselves from the international Communist movement. Therefore, it is up to the Yugoslav League of Communists to make a turn towards rapprochement with the Communist Parties on the basis of Marxism-Leninism; this would be also in the interests of the Yugoslav people themselves.

The Communist movement has dealt revisionism crushing blows. But revisionism is not dead yet. It must be borne in mind that imperialism will seek in every way to support and activize the revisionists.

There is also the need to combat dogmatism and sectarianism, which impede the development of Marxist-Leninist theory and its creative application and cause the Communist Parties to lose contact with the masses. Lenin's behest to strengthen the ties with the masses, to give the utmost heed to the voice of the masses and to march at the head of the masses is sacred to all us Communists.

As regards relations among the fraternal parties within the international Communist movement, we have always followed Lenin's presentation of the matter. Lenin taught us that these relations are erected upon the basis of equality and independence of the national detachments of the international working class, upon the principles of proletarian internationalism. It is precisely because all the Parties have equal rights that they have established relations of trust and voluntary cooperation, that as component units of the single great army of labor, they voluntarily and consciously seek united action.

All the Communist Parties are independent and work out their own policy, proceeding from the particular conditions in their respective countries; they have scored successes in their activity, are steadily extending their influence, increasing the number of their followers and winning prestige among all strata of the people.

The ideologists of imperialism and the revisionists who take their cue from them strive by every method to undermine the growing influence of the Communist Parties and spread the false assertion that the Communist movement is "the work of Moscow" and that the Communist and Workers' Parties are dependent upon the Communist Party of the Soviet Union. The Yugoslav revisionists, who allege that our party seeks "hegemonism" over other parties, show particular zeal. They have even included in their program the thesis of "hegemonism." The revisionists assert that our party interferes in the internal affairs of other countries and seeks to control the other Communist Parties. The reactionaries express particular gratefulness to the Yugoslav revisionists for this slander.

All who are familiar with the Communist movement will have no difficulty in smashing the falsehoods concocted by the international reactionaries and revisionists.

It is ridiculous to think that a political party of the working class, often numbering hundreds of thousands and sometimes millions of members, could be organized in any country from somewhere abroad. . . .

The Communist Parties arose not because some single center "planted" them in all countries. Such miracles do not happen. The history of the development of society shows that Marxist parties come into being with the appearance and growth of the working class. This means that the Communist movement arose as an objective necessity, that it was born of the very conditions of life of the working class in each country. There are classes in all the capitalist countries and consequently there are political parties of the working class and they will exist as long as the working class exists. In the same way, it is naive to think that the millions of people in the Communist Parties can be told from abroad what to think today and what to do tomorrow.

It is said that the "dependence" of the Communist and Workers' Parties on Moscow is corroborated by statements to the effect that the Communist Party of the Soviet Union stands at the head of the international Communist movement.

In making this claim, the well known thesis is cited from the declaration of the Moscow conference that "the camp of socialist states is headed by the Soviet Union."

The Communists of the Soviet Union and of all the other countries consider that this statement was a tribute to our country and the working class that, under the leadership of the Communist Party headed by the great Lenin, was the first to carry out the socialist revolution, the first to take power. In more than 40 years a long and difficult path of struggle and victories has been traversed and a powerful state, bulwark of all the socialist countries and of the world Communist movement, has been established.

We express sincere gratitude to the fraternal parties for this recognition of the historic role of the Soviet Union and the Communist Party of the Soviet Union.

At the same time, it must be emphasized that complete equality and independence have existed and do exist for all the Communist and Workers' Parties in the Communist movement and for the socialist countries in the socialist camp. In actuality the Communist Party of the Soviet Union does not control any parties, the Soviet Union does not control any other country. There are no "superior" or "subordinate" parties in the Communist movement. All the Communist and Workers' Parties are equal and independent, all of them bear responsibility for the destinies of the Communist movement, for its failures and successes. Each Communist or Workers' Party is responsible to the working class, to the working people, to its country, and to the whole international workers' and Communist movement. In the struggle for the interests of the working class, for socialism, the Communist Parties combine the universal tenets of Marxism-Leninism with the specific historical and national conditions in their countries. Only a Marxist-Leninist party connected with the working class, with the people of its country, is able to know the specific conditions of the struggle; it alone can work out a political line suiting these conditions and taking account of the traditions of the workers' movement of the given country.

And this is so in reality. All the Communist and Workers' Parties exist and struggle on the basis of complete independence and the principles of proletarian internationalism, of voluntary cooperation and mutual assistance. This is how our party understands the nature of the relations among the fraternal parties.

As regards the Soviet Union, its role, as is known, consists not in controlling other countries, but in having been the first to blaze the trail to socialism for mankind, in being the most powerful country in the international socialist system and the first to have entered the period of extensive building of communism. . . .

Figuratively speaking, our Communist Party regards itself as one of the advanced detachments of the world Communist movement, the detachment which is first to take the heights of communism. And on our way to these heights we shall not be stopped by an avalanche or landslide; nobody can make us turn off the path of advance toward communism.

We have always held and still hold that one cannot retire to one's national "domain" and withdraw into one's shell. We think that the might of the international Communist movement must be further reinforced in accordance with the principles adopted by all the fraternal parties in the Moscow declaration. Concern for the solidarity and strength of our ranks is the supreme internationalist duty of each Communist or Workers' Party. *Success in the national cause of the working class is inconceivable without the international solidarity of all its detachments.* . . .

In surveying the prospect of mankind's advance to communism, we must bear in mind the tremendous diversity of historical conditions in the different countries. Hence inevitably there arises a diversity of methods, ways and forms of applying the common laws of mankind's advance to communism. But, for all this, it must be emphasized that the principal, determining aspect in the development of all countries along the path to communism is the laws common to all of them, not the particular ways in which these laws are manifested. Marxism-Leninism requires the ability to apply the theory of scientific communism to the specific conditions of each individual country at the various stages of its development.

The Yugoslav leaders talk a great deal now about the

alleged fact that the Communist Parties are speaking out
against them because they, the Yugoslav leaders, take as
their starting point in building socialism the features
peculiar to their own country and do not follow the example and experience of other socialist countries. That,
of course, is a distortion of the truth. The Marxist-Leninist parties recognize that each country has its own
specific features of development. But this does not mean
that one can reach socialism by some other road that
lies to the side of the common path indicated by Marxism-Leninism. The particular features of the situation and
period in which one country or another is developing—
these must be taken into consideration. For example,
some measures applied in socialist construction in the Soviet Union in the past cannot be mechanically applied in
other countries. All the socialist countries are building
socialism, but they do not do it by stereotype.

The Communist Party of China is employing many
original forms of socialist construction. But we have no
disagreements with this party, nor can there be any
disagreements.

The Yugoslav revisionists are now concentrating their
fire on the Chinese People's Republic, disseminating all
sorts of inventions about alleged differences between the
Communist Parties of the Soviet Union and China. As
the Russian saying puts it, "the hungry man dreams of
bread." The revisionists are searching for discord among
our Communist Parties, but their illusory hopes are
doomed to failure. We are in full and complete agreement with the fraternal Communist Party of China, although in many respects its methods of building socialism do not resemble our own. We know that China
has its specific features of historical development, size of
population, level of production and national culture.
Therefore it would be a mistake to ignore these specific
features and to copy what is good for one country but
unsuitable for another.

Why have we no differences with the Communist Party
of China? Because we share the same class approach and
class conception. The Chinese Communist Party stands
firmly on Marxist-Leninist class positions. It is waging
a struggle against the imperialists and exploiters, a struggle to refashion life along socialist lines; it abides by the

principle of international proletarian solidarity and is guided by Marxist-Leninist theory.

The chief thing is to maintain and strengthen class solidarity in the struggle against capitalism, for the liberation of the working class, for the building of socialism. And on this score there is no divergence, there are no conflicting conceptions, among Communists, nor can there be. This is the main point that divides us from revisionists.

Part V

The Exposition
of Left-Wing Dogmatism

The formal acceptance by 12 Communist states in 1957 of a common action program under Soviet leadership had precluded the raising of theoretical issues that might threaten the unity of the camp or give the appearance of a public challenge to the Soviet position. While the self-isolation of Yugoslavia had furthered initially the prevailing tendency to oppose individual dissension by a united condemnation, the subsequent treatment of the Yugoslavian problem raised new issues of a fundamental nature. The Peking party obviously thought that the rather half-hearted economic sanctions applied by the Soviet Union against Yugoslavia represented an ineffective response to Revisionism. More significantly, the Chinese apparently also assumed some Soviet responsibility for the genesis of Yugoslav Revisionism. The new directions of Soviet policy since February 1956 had shown considerable tolerance toward national policies that deviated considerably from the fundamental requirements for the building of a Socialist society. From the Soviet point of view, adherence to the Moscow-directed camp took precedence over the individual members' approach to the indigenous development of Socialism.

To the Chinese, engaged at this time in the commune experiment, such Soviet policies represented a watering-down of Marxism-Leninism. No less objectionable, because here also Soviet policies appeared to be based on a lowering of the standards of the international class struggle, were Khrushchev's attempts to seek accommodation with the West through a series of summit meetings. The early endorsement of the summit approach in the joint Chinese-Soviet statement of August 1958 must be contrasted with the warnings issued about the futility of this device by the Chinese speaker at the Warsaw Pact meeting, some months prior to the 1960 summit meeting.

It is at this time—in February 1960 in Moscow, and in June 1960 in Bucharest—that the Chinese challenge, in face to face confrontation, the legitimacy in terms of Marxism of Soviet policies. The largely East-European audience on both occasions must have been unresponsive enough to the Chinese allegations to persuade them to use a friendlier domestic forum for the continuation of the debate. By the end of the summer of 1960, Yugoslav intervention in the dispute assisted a rapprochement between Moscow and Peking.

— 14 —

LONG LIVE LENINISM!
April, 1960*

. . . A speech by Tito at the end of last year referred repeatedly to the so-called new epoch of the modern revisionists. He said: "Today the world has entered an epoch in which nations can relax and tranquilly devote themselves to their internal construction tasks." Then he added: "We have entered an epoch in which new questions are on the agenda, not questions of war and peace but questions of cooperation, economic and otherwise. And where economic cooperation is concerned, there is also the question of economic competition."

This renegade completely writes off the question of class contradictions and class struggle in this world, in an attempt to negate the consistent analysis by Marxist-Leninists that our epoch is the epoch of imperialism and proletarian revolution, and the epoch of the victory of socialism and communism.

But what is the real situation in the world? Can the exploited and oppressed people in the imperialist countries "relax?" Can the peoples of all the colonies and semi-colonies still under imperialist oppression "relax?" Has the armed intervention led by the U.S. imperialists in Asia, Africa, and Latin America become "tranquil?" . . .

* *Red Flag* (theoretical fortnightly published by the Central Committee of the Chinese Communist Party). The article was written by the editorial department of this journal.

What kind of "construction" is meant when they "devote themselves to their international construction tasks?" Everyone knows that there are different kinds of countries in the world today, and principally two types of countries with social systems fundamentally different in nature. One type belongs to the world socialist system, the other to the world capitalist system. Is Tito referring to the "internal construction tasks" of arms expansion which the imperialists are carrying out in order to oppress the peoples of their own countries and oppress the whole world? Or is it the "internal construction" carried out by socialism for the promotion of the people's happiness and the seeking of lasting world peace?

Is the question of war and peace no longer an issue? Does imperialism no longer exist, the exploiting system no longer exist, and therefore the question of war no longer exist? Or is it that there can be no question of war even if imperialism and the exploiting system are allowed to survive forever?

The fact is that since World War II there has been continuous and unbroken warfare. Do not the imperialist wars to suppress national liberation movements and the imperialist wars of armed intervention against revolutions in various countries count as wars? Even though these wars have not developed into world wars, still do not these local wars count as wars? . . .

What kind of "cooperation" is meant? Is it "cooperation" of the proletariat with the bourgeoisie to protect capitalism? Is it "cooperation" of the colonial and semicolonial peoples with the imperialists to protect colonialism? Is it "cooperation" of socialist countries with capitalist countries to protect the imperialist system in its oppression of the peoples in these countries and suppression of national liberation wars?

In a word, the assertions of the modern revisionists about their so-called epoch are so many challenges to Leninism on the foregoing issues. It is their aim to obliterate the contradiction between the masses of people and the monopoly capitalist class in the imperialist countries, the contradiction between the colonial and semicolonial peoples and the imperialist aggressors, the contradiction between the socialist system and the imperialist system, and

the contradiction between the peace-loving people of the
world and the warlike imperialist bloc.

There are different ways of describing the distinction
between different "epochs." Generally speaking, there is
one way which is just drivel, concocting and manipulating
vague, ambiguous phrases and thus covering up the essence of the epoch. This is the old trick of the imperialists, the bourgeoisie, and the revisionists in the workers'
movement.

Then there is another way, which is making a concrete
analysis of the concrete situation with regard to class
contradictions and the class struggle, coming forward
with strictly scientific definitions, and thus bringing the
essence of the epoch thoroughly to light. This is the
work of every serious Marxist. . . .

Lenin always demanded that we examine the concrete
process of historical development on the basis of class
analysis, instead of talking vaguely about "society in
general" or "progress in general." We Marxists must not
base proletarian policy merely on certain passing events
or minute political changes, but must base it on the over-
all class contradictions and class struggles of a whole
historical epoch. This is a basic theoretical position of
Marxists. . . .

Contrary, however, to this series of revolutionary
Marxist statements, in the so-called new epoch of the
Titos, there is actually no imperialism, no proletarian
revolution, and, needless to say, no theory and policy of
the proletarian revolution and proletarian dictatorship.
In short, with them, the fundamental focal points of the
class contradictions and class struggles of our epoch are
nowhere to be seen, the fundamental questions of Leninism are absent, and there is no Leninism.

The modern revisionists insist that, in their so-called
new epoch, because of the progress of science and technology, the "old concepts" of Marx and Lenin are no
longer applicable. Tito made the following assertions:
"We are not dogmatists, for Marx and Lenin did not
predict the rocket on the moon, atomic bombs and the
great technical progress."

Not dogmatists, that's fine! Who wants them to be
dogmatists? But there is opposition to dogmatism on behalf of Marxism-Leninism and then there is nominal op-

position to dogmatism which is actually opposition to Marxism-Leninism. The Titos belong to the latter category. On the question of what effect scientific and technical progress has on social development, there are people who hold incorrect views because they are not able to approach the question from the materialist viewpoint of history. This is understandable. But the modern revisionists, on the other hand, are deliberately creating confusion on this question in a vain attempt to make use of the progress of science and technology to overthrow Marxism-Leninism. . . .

Unlike the bellicose imperialists, the socialist countries and peace-loving people the world over actively and firmly stand for the banning and destroying of atomic and nuclear weapons. We are always struggling against imperialist war, for the banning of atomic and nuclear weapons, and for the defense of world peace.

The more broadly and profoundly this struggle is waged, the more fully and thoroughly the brutish faces of bellicose U.S. imperialists and other imperialists are exposed, the more we will be able to isolate the United States and other imperialists before the people of the world, the greater will be the possibility of tying their hands, and the better it will be for the cause of world peace.

If, however, we lose our vigilance against the danger of the imperialists' launching a war, and do not work to arouse the people of all countries to rise up against imperialism but tie the hands of the people, then imperialism can prepare for war just as it pleases and the inevitable result will be an increase in the danger of the imperialists' launching a war. And, once war breaks out, the people may not be able quickly to adopt a correct attitude towards war because of complete lack of preparation or inadequate preparation, and thus will be unable to vigorously check the war.

Of course, whether or not the imperialists will unleash a war is not determined by us; we are, after all, not chiefs of staff to the imperialists. As long as the people of all countries raise their awareness and are fully prepared, with the socialist camp also making modern weapons, it can be definitely stated that if the United States or other imperialists refuse to reach an agreement on the

banning of atomic and nuclear weapons, the result will
be the very speedy destruction of those monsters under
the encirclement of the people the world over. And the
result will certainly not be annihilation of mankind.

We consistently oppose the launching of criminal wars
by imperialism, because an imperialist war would visit
enormous sacrifices upon the peoples of various countries—including the peoples of the United States and
other imperialist countries. But should the imperialists
insist on imposing such sacrifices on the people, we believe that, just as the experience of the Russian and Chinese revolutions show, those sacrifices would be repaid.
On the debris of a dead imperialism, the victorious people
would create with extreme rapidity a civilization thousands of times higher than the capitalist system and a
truly beautiful future for themselves.

The conclusion can only be this: Whichever way you
look at it, none of the new techniques, such as atomic
energy, rocketry, and the like, has changed the basic
characteristic of either the epoch of imperialism or proletarian revolution pointed out by Lenin, as alleged by the
modern revisionists. The capitalist-imperialist system absolutely will not crumble of itself. It will be pushed over
by the proletarian revolution within the imperialist country concerned, and the national revolution in the colonial
and semicolonial countries. The contemporary technical
progress cannot save the capitalist-imperialist system from
its doom, but will only ring a new death knell for it.

The modern revisionists, proceeding from their assured dictum on the current world situation and from
their assured dictum that "the Marxist-Leninist theory of
class analysis and class struggle is obsolete," attempt to
overthrow totally the fundamental theories of Marxism-
Leninism on a series of questions like violence, war,
peaceful coexistence, etc. There are also some people who
are not revisionists, but well-intentioned persons who
sincerely want to be Marxists, but are confused in the
face of certain new historical phenomena and thus have
some incorrect ideas. For example, some of them say
that the failure of the U.S. imperialists' policy of atomic
blackmail marks the end of violence. While thoroughly
refuting the absurdities of the modern revisionists, we

should also help these well-intentioned people to correct their erroneous ideas. . . .

The socialist world system has obviously gained the upper hand in its struggle with the capitalist world system. This great historic fact has weakened imperialism's position of violence in the world. But will this fact cause the imperialists to never again oppress the people of their own country, never again carry on outward expansion and aggressive activities? Can it make the warlike circles of the imperialists "lay down the butcher knife" and "sell their knives and buy oxen?" Can it make the groups of munitions merchants in the imperialist countries change over to peaceful pursuits? All these questions confront every serious Marxist-Leninist, and require deep consideration. It is obvious that whether these questions are viewed and handled correctly or incorrectly has a close bearing on the success or failure of the proletarian cause and the destiny of world humanity.

War is the most acute form of expression of violence. One type is civil war, another is foreign war. Violence is not always expressed by war, the most acute form. In capitalist countries, bourgeois war is the continuation of the bourgeois policies of ordinary times, while bourgeois peace is the continuation of bourgeois wartime policy. The bourgeoisie are always switching back and forth between the two forms, war and peace, to carry out their rule over the people and their external struggle. In what they call peacetime, the imperialists rely on armed force to deal with the oppressed classes and nations by such forms of violence as arrest, imprisonment, sentencing to hard labor, massacre, and so forth, while, at the same time, they also carry on preparations for using the most acute form of violence—war—to suppress the revolution of the people at home, to carry out plunder abroad, to overwhelm foreign competitors, and to stamp out revolutions in other countries. Or it may be that peace at home coexists with war abroad. . . .

True, some new questions have now arisen concerning peaceful coexistence. Confronted with the powerful Soviet Union and the powerful socialist camp, the imperialists must, at any rate, carefully consider whether they would not hasten their own extinction, as Hitler did, or bring about the most serious consequences for the capitalist system itself, if they should attack the Soviet Union, and/or attack the socialist countries. . . .

The foreign policy of socialist countries can only be a policy of peace. The socialist system determines that we do not need war, absolutely would not start a war, and absolutely must not, should not, and could not encroach one inch on the territory of a neighboring country. Ever since its founding, the People's Republic of China has adhered to a foreign policy of peace. Our country, together with two neighboring countries, India and Burma, jointly initiated the well-known Five Principles of Peaceful Coexistence; and at the Bandung Conference of 1955 our country, together with various countries of Asia and Africa, adopted the 10 Principles of Peaceful Coexistence.

The Communist Party and government of our country have in the past few years consistently supported the activities carried out by the Central Committee of the Communist Party and the Government of the Soviet Union headed by Comrade N. S. Khrushchev on behalf of peace, considering that these activities on the part of the Government and the Communist Party of the Soviet Union have further demonstrated before the people of the world the firmness of the socialist countries' peaceful foreign policy, as well as the need for the people to keep the imperialists from launching another world war and to strive for a lasting world peace. . . .

So long as there is a continuous development of these mighty forces, it is possible to maintain the situation of peaceful coexistence, or even to obtain some sort of official agreement on peaceful coexistence or to conclude an agreement on prohibition of atomic and nuclear weapons. That would be a fine thing in full accord with the aspirations of the peoples of the world. However, under these circumstances, as long as the imperialist system still exists, the most acute form of violence—namely, war—has by no means ended in the world. The fact is not as depicted by the Yugoslav revisionists, who say Lenin's definition that "war is the continuation of politics," which he repeatedly elucidated and persisted in while combating opportunism, is obsolete.

We believe in the absolute correctness of Lenin's thinking: War is an inevitable outcome of exploiting systems, and the source of modern wars is the imperialist system. Until the imperialist system and the exploiting classes come to an end, wars of one kind or another will always appear. They may be wars among the imperialists for redivision of the world, or wars of aggression and anti-aggression between the imperialists and the oppressed nations, or civil wars of revolution and counterrevolution between the exploited and exploiting classes in the imperialist countries, or, of course, wars in which the imperialists attack the socialist countries and the socialist countries are forced to defend themselves.

All types of war represent the continuation of the policies of definite classes. Marxism-Leninism absolutely must not sink into the mire of bourgeois pacifism, and can only appraise all these kinds of wars and thus draw conclusions for proletarian policy by adopting the method of concrete class analysis. . . .

In a word, in the interests of the people of the world, we must thoroughly shatter the falsehoods of the modern revisionists and persist in the Marxist-Leninist viewpoints on the question of violence, war, and peaceful coexistence.

The Yugoslav revisionists deny the inherent class nature of violence and thereby obliterate the fundamental difference between revolutionary violence and counter-revolutionary violence; they deny the inherent class nature of war and thereby obliterate the fundamental difference between just war and unjust war; they deny that imperialist war is a continuation of imperialist policy, deny the danger of the imperialists' unleashing another big war, deny that it will be possible to do away with war only after doing away with the exploiting classes, and even shamelessly call the U.S. imperialist chieftain Eisenhower "the man who laid the cornerstone for eliminating the cold war and establishing lasting peace with peaceful competition between different political systems." They deny that, under the condition of peaceful coexistence, there are still complicated, acute struggles in the political, economic and ideological fields; and so on. All these arguments of the Yugoslav revisionists are aimed at poisoning the minds of the proletariat and the people of all countries, and are helpful to the imperialist policy of war.

Modern revisionists seek to confuse the peaceful foreign policy of the socialist countries with the domestic policies of the proletariat in the capitalist countries. They thus hold that peaceful coexistence between countries with different social systems means that capitalism can peacefully grow into socialism, that the proletariat in countries ruled by the bourgeoisie can renounce class struggle and can have "peaceful cooperation" with the bourgeoisie and the imperialists, and that the proletariat and all the exploited classes should forget the fact that they are living in a class society, and so on. All these views are also diametrically opposed to Marxism-Leninism. They are put forward in an attempt to protect imperialist rule and keep the proletariat and all the rest of the working people perpetually in capitalist enslavement.

Peaceful coexistence between nations and people's revolutions in various countries are by nature two different things, not the same thing; two different concepts, not one; two different kinds of questions, not the same kind of question. Peaceful coexistence refers to relations between different nations; revolution means the overthrow of the oppressors as a class by the oppressed people within a country, while in the case of the colonial and semi-colonial countries, it is, first and foremost, a question of the overthrow of alien oppressors—namely, the imperialists. Before the October Revolution, the question of peaceful coexistence between socialist and capitalist countries did not exist, as there were as yet no socialist countries in the world; but there did exist at that time the questions of the proletarian revolution and the national revolution, as the peoples in various countries, in accordance with their own specific conditions, had long put revolutions of one or the other kind on the agenda of the day to settle the destinies of their countries.

We are Marxist-Leninists. We have always considered that the question of revolution is a nation's own affair. We have always held that the working class can only depend on itself for its emancipation, and that the emancipation of the people of any country depends on their own political consciousness and on the ripening of revolutionary conditions in that country. Revolution can neither be exported nor imported. No one can prevent the people of a foreign country from carrying out a revolution, nor can one manufacture a revolution in a foreign country as if "helping the rice shoots to grow by pulling them up." . . .

When a socialist country, in the face of imperialist aggression, is compelled to launch counterattacks in a defensive war, and goes beyond its own border to pursue and eliminate its enemies from abroad, as the Soviet Union did in the war against Hitler, is this justified? Certainly it is completely justified, absolutely necessary and entirely just. In accordance with the strict principles of communists, such operations by the socialist countries must be strictly limited to the time when the imperialists launch a war of aggression against them. Socialist countries never permit themselves to send, never should, and never will send their troops across their borders unless they are subjected to aggressive attack from a foreign enemy. Since the armed forces of the socialist countries fight for justice, when these forces have to go beyond their borders to counterattack a foreign enemy, it is only natural that they should exert an influence and have an effect wherever they go; but even then, the occurrence of people's revolutions and the establishment of the socialist system in those places and countries where they go will still depend on the will of the masses of the people there.

The spread of revolutionary ideas knows no national boundaries. But in a given country under given circumstances it is only through the efforts made by the people themselves that these ideas will yield revolutionary fruit. . . .

It would be in the best interests of the people if the proletariat could attain power and carry out the transition to socialism by peaceful means. It would be wrong to ignore such a possibility when it appears. Whenever the opportunity for the "peaceful development of the revolution" presents itself communists must seize it, as Lenin did, so as to realize the aim of the socialist revolution. The opportunity as such, however, is always, in Lenin's words, "an extraordinarily rare oportunity in the history of revolutions." When in a given country a certain local political power is already surrounded by revolutionary forces or when in the world a certain capitalist country is already surrounded by socialism, there might be a greater possibility for the peaceful development of the revolution. But even then, the peaceful development of the revolution should never be regarded as the only possibility and it is therefore necessary to be prepared at the same time for the other possibility; i.e., nonpeaceful development of the revolution.

. . . At a time when the imperialist countries and the imperialists are armed to the teeth as never before in order to protect their savage man-eating system, can it be said that the imperialists have become very "peaceable" towards the proletariat and the people at home and the oppressed nations abroad, as the modern revisionists suggest, and that, therefore, the "extraordinarily rare opportunity in the history of revolutions" which Lenin spoke about after the February revolution will become a normal state of affairs confronted by the world proletariat and all the oppressed people, and so that what Lenin referred to as a "rare opportunity" can be picked up anywhere by the proletariat in the capitalist countries? We hold that these views are completely groundless. . . .

So, contrary to the modern revisionists who seek to benumb the revolutionary will of the people by empty talk about peaceful transition, Marxist-Leninists hold that the question of the possibility of peaceful transition to socialism can be raised only in the light of the specific conditions in each country at a particular time. The proletariat must never allow itself to one-sidedly and groundlessly base its thinking, policy, and its whole work on the calculation that the bourgeoisie is willing to accept peaceful transformation. It must, at the same time, make two preparations: one for the peaceful development of the revolution and the other for the nonpeaceful development of the revolution. Whether the transition will be carried out through armed uprising or by peaceful means is a question that differs categorically from that of peaceful coexistence between the socialist and capitalist countries; it is an internal affair of each country, one to be determined only by the relative strength of the classes in that country in a given period; a matter to be decided only by the communists themselves of that country. . . .

At the beginning of the 20th century Lenin in "What Is To Be Done?" drew attention to the question that "the spread of Marxism was accompanied by a certain lowering of theoretical standards." Lenin cited Marx's opinion contained in a letter on "The Gotha Program" that we may enter into agreements to attain the practical aims of the movement, but we must never bargain over principles and make "concessions" in theory. . . .

. . . it is extremely important to adhere firmly to the revolutionary principles of Marxism-Leninism and to wage an irreconcilable struggle against any tendency to lower the standards of the revolution, especially against revisionism and right opportunism.

In regard to the question of safeguarding world peace at the present time there are also certain people who declare that ideological disputes are no longer necessary, or that there is no longer any difference in principle between communists and social democrats. This is tantamount to lowering the ideological and political standards of communists to those of the bourgeoisie and social democrats. Those who make such statements have been influenced by modern revisionism and have departed from the positions of Marxism-Leninism. . . .

"Peace" in the mouths of modern revisionists is intended to whitewash the war preparations of the imperialists, to play again the old tune of "ultra-imperialism" of the old opportunists, which was long since refuted by Lenin, and to distort our communist policy concerning peaceful coexistence between countries of two different systems into elimination of the people's revolution in various countries. It was that old revisionist Bernstein who made this shameful and notorious statement: "The movement is everything, the final aim is nothing."

The modern revisionists have a similar statement: The peace movement is everything, the final aim is nothing. Therefore, the "peace" they talk about is in practice limited to the "peace" which may be acceptable to the imperialists under certain historical conditions. It attempts to lower the revolutionary standards of the peoples of various countries and enervate their revolutionary will.

We communists are struggling for the defense of world

peace, for the realization of the policy of peaceful co-existence. Meanwhile we support the revolutionary wars of the oppressed nations against imperialism. We support the revolutionary wars of the oppressed peoples for their own liberation and social progress because all revolutionary wars are just wars. Naturally, we must continue to explain to the masses the viewpoint of Lenin concerning the capitalist imperialist system as the source of wars in modern times; we must continue to explain to the masses the Marxist-Leninist thesis on the replacement of capitalist imperialism by socialism and communism as the final goal of our struggle. We must not hide our principles before the masses. . . .

The declaration of the Moscow meeting pointed out that "the main danger at present is revisionism, or, in other words, rightwing opportunism." Some say that this judgement of the Moscow meeting no longer holds good under today's condition. We believe this statement to be wrong. It makes the people overlook the importance of the struggle against the main danger—revisionism—and is very harmful to the revolutionary cause of the proletariat. . . .

As pupils of Lenin and Leninists we must utterly smash all attempts of the modern revisionists to distort and carve up the teachings of Lenin. . . .

EXCERPTS FROM A *PRAVDA* ARTICLE DEFENDING KHRUSHCHEV'S POLICIES AGAINST CRITICS

June, 1960*

In July, 1920, leaders of the international workers' and Communist movement who arrived in Moscow for the Second Congress of the Communist International (Comintern) received copies of V. I. Lenin's book "Leftist Sectarianism, a Childhood Disease of Communism," which had just been published. . . .

Urgently cautioning the newly created Communist parties against the tricks of the agents of imperialism, Lenin also warned against another serious danger, Leftist sectarianism, which he called the childhood disease of Communism.

. . . Lenin devoted a large part of his book to a justification of the international significance of the Great October Socialist Revolution. Noting the historical inevitability of repeating on an international scale what had already been achieved and the influence of the Great October on the course of world history, Lenin stressed that "the Russian example shows all countries something that is very essential out of their inevitable and not-too-distant future."

In addition, Lenin called in his book for a creative approach from a Marxist viewpoint to all questions of social development. He spoke of the need to research, to study, to run down, to guess what is especially national, specifically national in each country for a solution of individual international tasks in the struggle for communism. . . .

* Current Digest of the Soviet Press, Vol. XII, No. 24. Reprinted by permission.

Present-day revisionists who ignore the general principles of the development of communism and who try to find their own course toward the establishment of socialism are concentrating their fire on the principles of Socialist construction in the U.S.S.R. and other Socialist countries, and are misinterpreting Lenin.

The search for a separate course to socialism for each country individually, the desire to build socialism on the basis of imperialist handouts or attempts to skip entire historic stages serve only the enemies of the working class interested in weakening socialism. Unmasking the false, anti-Marxist views of the advocates of "separate courses," Comrade N. S. Khrushchev said: "If such a point of view is adopted, it may well result in so many 'courses' that people will get lost, as in a forest, and will not know how to reach their goal. In life there is only a single, Leninist course toward the construction of socialism and communism, a course tested by his historical experience, the course of the Great October Socialist Revolution."

V. I. Lenin carefully cautioned the Communist and workers' parties against possible errors and taught them to be bold in uncovering and correcting any errors committed. To those questions Lenin devoted the second half of his book. It criticizes serious shortcomings in the activities of certain Communist parties. These shortcomings consisted of a lack of desire of several Communists who had been afflicted by the Leftist disorder to work in reactionary trade unions and to participate in parliaments and of their rejection of possible compromises.

V. I. Lenin demonstrated the unsoundness and harm of the slogans of the Leftists who rejected the idea of Communist compromises with other parties and groups. He said that the Leftists, though considering themselves Marxists, had forgotten the fundamental truths of Marxism. Vladimir Ilyich (Lenin) recalled a statement by F. Engels who once criticized the Blanquists (followers of Blanqui, an early French Communist) for wanting to skip through all intermediate stages directly to communism without taking account of the new historical development, and remarked that if power will be in their hands, "communism will be introduced" the day after tomorrow. Engels described as childish naivete the Blanquists' attempts to put forward their own impatience as a theoretically convincing argument.

"Naïve and utterly inexperienced people," Lenin wrote, "imagine that it is sufficient to admit the permissibility of compromises in general in order to obliterate the dividing line between opportunism, against which we wage and must wage an uncompromising struggle, and revolutionary Marxism or communism.

"But if such people do not yet know that all dividing lines in nature and in society are mutable and, to a certain extent, conditional, they cannot be assisted in any way other than by a long process of training, education, enlightenment, political and everyday experience."

Creatively developing Marxist-Leninist theory under the new conditions and generalizing the great experience of Socialist construction in our country in full accordance with the principles of social development, the twenty-first party congress laid out a well-grounded, full-fledged program for the transition from socialism to communism. That program is the concrete embodiment of the general line of the Communist party in the present stage.

Characterizing the process of transition from socialism to communism, Comrade N. S. Khrushchev told the twenty-first party congress:

"We must not hurry and hastily introduce what has not yet matured. That would lead to distortions and compromise our cause. But neither must we rest on our laurels because such a course would lead to stagnancy."

The course of social development is objective. We consider erroneous and incorrect the statements of Leftists in the international Communist movement to the effect that since we have taken power into our hands we can at once introduce communism by-passing certain historic stages in its development. Such statements are contrary to Leninism. Lenin taught us that to try to anticipate the result of a fully developed, fully consolidated and established, fully unfolded and matured communism amounts to the same thing as to try to teach higher mathematics to a four-year-old child.

The left-sectarian sentiments and tendencies against which Lenin's book is leveled find their manifestation here and there even in our day. Some people mistakenly regard the policy of working for the peaceful coexistence of countries with different political systems, of struggling to put an end to the arms race and to strengthen peace and friendship among peoples, and of talks between the leaders of the socialist and capitalist countries as a kind of departure from the positions of Marxism-Leninism. . . .

Lenin taught that it is impossible to wage the highly complex struggle for communism, the struggle with the international bourgeoisie, if one begins by rejecting agreements and compromises on specific problems with possible, albeit temporary and unstable, allies and by rejecting the exploitation of even temporarily conflicting interests among enemies. While in certain cases accepting compromises for the sake of the development of the revolutionary movement, Communists never allow retreats from their fundamental positions. "In questions of ideology," Comrade N. S. Khrushchev has said, "we have stood and shall stand firm as a rock on the foundation of Marxism-Leninism."

Throughout this work of Lenin's there runs like a red thread the idea that work with the masses is a task of vital importance for each party. Without flexible and intelligent tactics, without the ability to harness all forms and facets of public activity, the masses cannot be won over or victory gained; it is essential that we know how to uphold the interests of the revolution in non-revolutionary institutions as well. . . .

Great creative enthusiasm has been evident in the life of the Communist Parties in recent years. True to Lenin's behests, the fraternal parties have been creatively developing and applying Marxist-Leninist theory in present-day circumstances. A great contribution to the further development of Marxism-Leninism was made by our party at its 20th and 21st Congresses. The elaboration by the Congresses of such fundamental problems as the peaceful coexistence and competition of the two systems, the possibility of preventing wars in the contemporary epoch, the forms of transition of various countries to socialism, and ways of strengthening the world socialist system is of the greatest significance for international life. The decisions of the 20th and 21st Congresses of the C.P.S.U. received the unanimous endorsement of the Communist and Workers' Parties.

All the basic propositions of Lenin's book are vital at
the present time. They are leveled against rightist opportunists, present-day revisionists and leftist doctrinaires.
The Communist Parties, while regarding revisionism as
the primary danger, at the same time draw attention to
sectarianism and dogmatism, which may also represent
a great danger at particular stages in the development
of this or that party.

— 16 —

SOCIALISM AND WAR: A SURVEY OF CHINESE CRITICISM OF THE POLICY OF COEXISTENCE

Edvard Kardelj, 1960*

For a considerable time now, the columns of the
Chinese press and the speeches of many official Chinese
spokesmen—including even the highest state and party
leaders—have been full of all sorts of attacks on Yugoslavia's foreign policy, and particularly on our concepts
of peaceful, active coexistence of states with differing
social systems.

It is obvious that the pressure of these Chinese attacks is directed against the entire front of the international policy of present-day socialism with the aim of
extorting certain precise solutions of the dilemma
which faces the forces of socialism in the present-day
world. . . .

CHINESE IDEOLOGY AND CHINESE REALITY

If from a mass of empty words, slanders, verbalist
dialectics and general political slogans we extract the
real substance of the Chinese charges against Yugoslav

* Publishing House Jugoslavija, Belgrade, 1960.

foreign policy, they boil down to the following basic arguments.

The first argument asserts: the Yugoslav communists are revisionists and their revisionism derives from their fear of imperialism and war. This cowardice of theirs has persuaded them to pursue an opportunist policy of compromise with the bourgeoisie and with imperialism. Thereby, they have sunk from the position of a revolutionary settlement of accounts with capitalism to that of reformism and now accept the theory of the peaceful growing of capitalism into socialism. To conceal this, the Yugoslav communists embellish imperialism. Consequently, they assist American imperialism. To that end they have even invented the policy of active coexistence, which is nothing less than a device for the concealment of their opportunist policy.

The second argument says: in contradistinction to this Yugoslav "opportunism," Chinese communists are not afraid either of imperialism or of war. They are for a radical settlement of accounts between the world of socialism and that of imperialism by means of a revolutionary clash. If this is war, it will be a just war and one should not be afraid of it or renounce it, because the sacrifices will soon be recompensed.

Further, the Chinese communists say that the assertion of the possibility of any lasting coexistence between the world of socialism and the world of capitalism and imperialism is illusory and harmful.

They consider that sooner or later a conflict between these two worlds is inevitable. As these Chinese authors see it, there can be talk of coexistence, disarmament, the policy of agreement, and so forth, solely for the purpose of unmasking imperialism. On the other hand, to take the principle of coexistence to be a lasting and essential principle of socialist international policy would according to these conceptions be tantamount to renouncing the revolutionary method of resolution of the social contradictions of the present-day world. To speak today about peaceful means of struggle for a transition from capitalism to socialism, that is, to the rule of the working-class is, according to those conceptions, not only unrealistic—as the proletariat can never overcome counterrevolutionary violence otherwise than by means of revolutionary violence—but also senseless and opportunist, for at a time when the strength of the socialist countries is growing so rapidly, these countries should not renounce the possibility of settling accounts with imperialism in a revolutionary way, and should not run away from war.

If we reduce these arguments to what is fundamental—as seen through Chinese spectacles—we get the following picture: the Yugoslav communists are opportunists, whereas the Chinese communists are radical revolutionaries.

At the first glance it is clear that this picture reflects a highly simplified and sectarian understanding of the Marxist postulates about the socialist revolution. Further, it is obvious that in some cases these "genuine Marxists" of China have only been concerned to bother about Marxism to the extent necessary for the successful application of a familiar and indeed notorious method of unprincipled struggle.

Let us now, in contradistinction to this cooked-up piece of chinese "ideology," glance at the facts and make an attempt to elucidate the real essence of the differences of opinion on matters of socialist international policy, not excluding either the question of the so-called peaceful transition to socialism, which for quite definite reasons the Chinese theoreticians—and not we—tie up with those differences of opinion.

Here the first thing we have to do is to draw attention to the fact that the authors of these Chinese attacks on our policy make great efforts to lend those attacks the appearance of ideological and theoretical differences of opinion about Marxism. This is a device as hypocritical as it is anti-Marxist. By it, in fact, the Chinese critics of Yugoslavia are—both deliberately and unwittingly—striving to conceal the real, material essence of the matter. . . .

. . . when the Chinese theoreticians—criticising the foreign policies of other socialist countries from a "Marxist" standpoint, try to impose their conceptions of socialist international policy upon others, they do so as a claim to be the monopolistic interpreters of "true" Marxism. But in fact, all they do is force their policy upon others, a policy which is the result of specific

Chinese social conditions, which in this case are not in harmony with the ideological aims of socialism. For the very method by which this policy is being forced upon others—of which the Chinese anti-Yugoslav campaign is the most eloquent evidence—points to the fact that the authors of this campaign are striving for a monopolistic leading role, ideological and political, in the socialist world, precisely in order to subordinate the interests of world socialism to their own political interests.

ON THE INEVITABILITY OF WAR

It is utterly un-Marxist and unscientific when the Chinese theoreticians argue their thesis about the inevitability of war by the generalised scheme—capitalism inevitable war, socialism inevitable peace, therefore peace is feasible only if capitalism is completely eliminated. The problem can only be grasped completely if the concrete material and political factors and the quantitative relationships which at any given moment are decisive for war or peace are analysed as well as the prospects of their further development. Looked at in the abstract, the inevitability of war has never been absolute, fatal. It has always depended on the relationship of forces. And when Lenin drew the conclusion that under the conditions of imperialism war was inevitable, because the imperialist factors inevitably "bred" war, what he was really thinking of was a relationship of forces in which the imperialist forces were superior, if not infinitely superior. Consequently it was precisely a certain relationship of forces which made war inevitable in the circumstances of the absolute domination of imperialism. Whoever fails to grasp this is also unable to see that the struggle for peace is in the circumstances of today precisely one of the means of struggle for *further change in the relationship of forces* in favour of peace and socialism, not for the petrification of the present relationship of forces. This, of course, supposing peace to be in the elementary interest of socialism, which the Chinese theoreticians also question. . . .

War is inevitable if the forces of peace are too weak to prevent it. War can be prevented if the forces of peace overcome the forces of war. Consequently, *to speak of the inevitability of war—from the standpoint of Marxism—means one thing only: an objective appraisal that*

the relationship of forces between reaction and imperi
ism on the one hand and the working-class and the an
imperialist forces on the other is such that this latter fe
tor is unable to prevent war. . . .

When they make their mechanical defence of the fo
mula that "war is inevitable," do the Chinese critics ma
such a factual analysis of the relationship of forces th
starting point? No, they do not even mention it. In th
regard they are satisfied with the propaganda phrase th
imperialism is a "paper tiger." Consequently, their stu
born insistence that this "paper tiger" will neverthele
inevitably begin a war against the socialist camp sim
taneously shows that they have not even got faith in th
own propagandist phrase. . . .

. . . the differences of opinion regarding the theo
about the inevitability of war . . . before all else ha
a deeper root in one or other of the two following po
sibilities:

> either the Chinese theoreticians believe that the relationsh
> of forces in the world is such that the factors of imperiali
> not merely wish to impose war on the world, with prospe
> of winning, but are also capable of doing so;

> or the Chinese theoreticians consider that war is in the
> terests of socialism, that is to say, that it is the "revo
> tionary weapon" of socialism, and consequently the grov
> of the forces of socialism of itself makes war inevitab

In the first instance, over-estimating the forces of i
perialism, they deny their own theory about the "pap
tiger." In the second case they are venturing on to a ve
dangerous and very slippery road, which leads to t
complete deformation of socialist international poli
and of the relationship between the nations on the s
cialist road.

. . . let us return to the analysis of the quantitati
relationship of the social forces and the influence of the
on the problem of the inevitability of war. Through t
prism of those relationships let us examine all three po
sible forms of imperialist war.

From the standpoint of military techniques and
other conditions, war for the conquest of other peopl
is still not only possible but, in certain conditions, re
tively the least risky for the aggressor. Neverthele

practical examples of this phenomenon indicate that the possibilities of such wars and the chances of success in them are becoming increasingly less. This is unquestionably the consequence of the growth of anti-imperialist resistance among the oppressed peoples, of a strengthening of the feeling of national independence and of equality, and a strengthening of the socialist forces and their support and of democratic resistance within the capitalist countries. We can with justice assume that all these anti-imperialist factors will grow stronger, and this means that in future it will be increasingly more difficult to start even local wars for the enslavement of other peoples.

The second kind of imperialist war, that is, war between the large imperialist states themselves, waged for a new division of the world, to all intents became obsolete during the Second World War. However the imperialist contradictions inside the capitalist world develop in future, the basic contradiction of the world of today—the contradiction between the world of socialism and the world of capitalism—has to such an extent reduced them to the state of being a secondary factor that the possibility of wars breaking out between the large capitalist countries for a new share-out of the world has been reduced to a theoretical minimum such that in political practice it scarcely needs considering.

By this, it goes without saying, I do not mean to assert that capitalist contradictions no longer exist. They do exist, but they are so weakened, and the forms through which they manifest themselves are so changed, that they are no longer capable alone, independently, of being resolved by war—except in various forms of wars on other people's backs—but are instead connected up with the basic contradiction of the world of today, the contradiction between socialism and capitalism. . . .

And finally, the third kind of imperialist war—an aggressive war against the socialist states. Such a war is not only possible, but even has its protagonists in the most reactionary and war-mongering circles of the capitalist world. Admittedly, among them there are not very many who would be openly for war under present-day conditions, for the majority of them are aware that today aggressive war has no prospects of achieving. But there are many more who, like the Chinese communists, consider war inevitable, so continue to keep the iron hot in the fire, in the hope that time will change things to their advantage.

However, counter to those tendencies and circles there also exists all that tremendous material and political strength of the factors of peace, progress, socialism in the world and inside those countries of which we spoke above. There is no reason whatsoever to envisage these factors becoming weaker in the future. On the contrary, they will grow stronger and develop an increasingly powerful influence on the course of world events. To believe that in such circumstances war is inevitable is either to over-estimate the force of the factor of imperialism very seriously or very seriously to under-estimate the strength of socialism and of the other anti-imperialist factors.

We do neither. We are not inclined to under-estimate the strength of the imperialist factors. For this reason we consider it the indispensable duty of all nations and all peace-loving forces to struggle actively for peace and for the suppression of all aggressive tendencies. But we are also not inclined to under-estimate the strength of the progress and peace-loving factors, which are becoming ever more capable of eliminating any chance of the aggressor's succeeding in a war.

In other words, for war to cease to be inevitable it is not necessary for the last corner of the world to be socialist, *but for the material and ethical-political forces of socialism and peace to be so strong that they are able to prevent any attempt to resolve the imperialist and other international contradictions by war, which will at the same time speed up the attempt to resolve those contradictions by internal means and internal forms of political and economic struggle within every country.*

What support then remains for the Chinese theory of the inevitability of war at the present time? There remains only one more theoretical possibility, the supposition that the socialist countries might adopt the line of finding a solution to the contradiction between the world of socialism and the world of capitalism by war. This would mean the deliberate adoption by the socialist countries of a policy of a war of conquest. However, such trends would both ideologically and in practice be in complete opposition to the aims of socialism and its elementary interests both today and tomorrow. For this reason there is little likelihood of their finding support in the socialist world, which we can best see from the fortune of the theories of the Chinese authors which we are discussing here. . . .

In circumstances when the socialist system has become a world force, but within its framework still exist vestiges of the old views and egotistic and other tendencies, the phenomenon is not excluded that some country on the socialist road—because of certain specific inner conditions—yields to the temptation to make use of the strength of socialism, not only for its defence but also for an attempt to achieve certain aims which have no connection whatsoever with socialism. Consequently, proportionately to the growth of the power of the socialist countries also grows their responsibility for peace, the responsibility of all the socialist forces.

At the present time material and social-political conditions are increasingly maturing which prevent war. If such possibilities exist, the socialist forces have only one choice—to struggle to see that possibility exploited to the utmost, that is, for peace to be preserved. For this reason they must oppose those trends within the socialist world which act in the opposite direction, and among these is not only the anti-communist campaign of certain social-democratic circles, but also such a campaign against the very policy of coexistence, and against Yugoslavia in particular such as—with a line asserting the inevitability of war—the leading circles of the Communist Party of China lead. . . .

THE POLICY OF COEXISTENCE AND MARXISM

The problem of the feasibility or nonfeasibility of the policy of coexistence is closely connected in the first place with the question of how far the proposition is realistic which says that today wars are no longer inevitable. If war is inevitable, coexistence is an unfeasible fiction, an illusion. In other words, proving that war is inevitable is simultaneously to prove that the policy of coexistence is unfeasible, consequently is mistaken and harmful to the cause of socialism. And indeed, in the work of Chinese theoreticians today we do find, appropriately enough, this very argument further buttressed by appeals to "true"

Marxism. And the target of attack in this question is Yugoslavia, so that Yugoslavia should be used for a political battle waged generally against the policy of peaceable coexistence and peace.

At times the Chinese authors, in words, are in favour of peaceable coexistence, but not in favour of the same sort of coexistence as the Yugoslav communists. . . .

Real differences of opinion of course do exist. But they do not reside in any conception of the "quality" of coexistence, but in the fact that the Yugoslav communists stand for a policy of coexistence, while the arguments of the Chinese theoreticians show that in reality they are against it. According to the Chinese theoreticians the sin of the Yugoslavs is in the fact that they assert that the policy of coexistence is a lasting one, a fundamental element of socialist international policy, while in the Chinese view coexistence can be no more than a transitory state, which sooner or later will be terminated either by imperialism or by the socialist forces, which have no reason fundamentally to renounce war for the destruction of imperialism. In addition to this, of course, these critics add that the Yugoslav policy of coexistence amounts to propaganda for the *status quo* between the enslavers and the enslaved, the exploiters and the exploited and so forth, while of their own "policy of coexistence" they assert that it is based on the future revolutionary collapse of imperialism, for which reason it is equally inevitably a transitory policy, a temporary one, seeing that a war against imperialism is inevitable.

. . . As is known, for Yugoslav communists the justification of the policy of coexistence is based on the following:

1) on the conviction that in the circumstances of today it will be increasingly more difficult for the forces of imperialism and war to break the existing coexistence, while this will bring the internal contradictions and oppositions of the capitalist world to a new stage of development, that is, it will speed up the processes of distintegration of imperialism and capitalism as a system and increasingly strengthen the part played by socialist factors, material and political;

2) on the conviction that the imposing of socialism on other nations from outside by war is a harmful and profoundly anti-socialist conception, behind which can be—

and inevitably will be—hidden all manner of hegemonistic and reactionary trends, apart from which the socialist countries' assumption of responsibility for a frightfully destructive world war, in order by force to "make others happy" would profoundly compromise the very concept of socialism and lend imperialism and all the vestiges of the old world new strength.

In other words, *the policy of coexistence is the expression of our conviction that in the circumstances of today war-mongering circles in the capitalist world are going to have ever less feasibility of forcing a new world war on mankind, while the socialist world in principle and in practice rejects, or should reject, the very notion of a war of conquest as the instrument for forcing socialism on others.* Since we conceive of the policy of coexistence in this way, it of course must necessarily be a permanent principle of socialist international policy or not be at all. . . .

ON THE INEVITABILITY OF ARMED REVOLUTION

For the sense of the Chinese line of war's being inevitable to be completely clear, we need to examine yet another theory on which the Chinese theoreticians insist, the theory about the inevitability of forcible methods, that is to say, of an armed uprising, or revolutionary war, in every country. For this too they found exclusively on specially selected and crookedly presented quotations from the classics of Marxism and Leninism, and not on an analysis of the objective facts.

Here two things call for elucidation, namely, what is the point of including that theory in a discussion about peace and coexistence, and what connection has this theory with Marxism or Leninism? . . .

In fact, this thesis, beside the thesis about the inevitability of war, is an additional foundation stone of the theory that the policy of coexistence is an untenable one. For from this thesis they draw the logical conclusion that if in more or less every country in the world the armed form of revolution and the same forms of the dictatorship of the proletariat are essential for the transition from capitalism to socialism to be accomplished, then any talk of coexistence is a reactionary act which holds up the revolutionary showdown, whereas war between the socialist and the capitalist world in fact would mean not only the speeding up of that development, but also itself become a form of the "world revolution." The final conclusion logically to be drawn obligatorily from such a thesis is that not only should we not struggle against war, but we should desire it, since it is precisely war that speeds up the course of the world socialist revolution. . . .

ON JUST AND UNJUST WAR

Yet another theory plays a fairly large part in the Chinese critique of Yugoslav foreign policy and the policy of coexistence as such, namely, a theory about just and unjust war. It is only when we subject that theory too to examination that we obtain a complete picture of the Chinese notions about a socialist international policy in the present time.

The sense of this theory, as explained by the Chinese theoreticians, might be formulated in the following way: since wars are divided into just and unjust wars, communists are not against all wars, they are only against unjust wars, and if a war is just, they cannot be against it, for that would be to pact with evil, with imperialism, it would be opportunism, withdrawal from a revolutionary stand. Thus here logic is turned upside down.

For the ultimate consequence and simultaneously the explanation of this thesis would be that since war between the world of capitalism and the world of socialism, as the ineluctable form of resolution of contradictions in the "international class struggle," is inevitable and in addition is from the standpoint of socialism just, revolutionary, one should not struggle against it. What is more, to struggle against it is in the spirit of this logic just as wrong as it would be wrong to struggle against the revolution in any individual country.

To all these arguments, of course, is tied a string of accusations and slanders against the Yugoslav communists, such as that they make no distinction between just and unjust war, that "like all pacifists" they are against any war and that this means pacting with imperialism, renunciation of aid to oppressed peoples who are struggling for independence, and so on.

I have no intention of spending time on these accusations and slanders.

Today beside the capitalist states there are also socialist states, with their armies, their military technology, their economic strength. The contradictions are concentrated as between these two great camps. Here the question is not whether war between these two camps would be just or not, but whether the leading socialist forces should adopt the line of trying to resolve those contradictions by war or by other means, that is, by the internal social processes. *This means that the concrete problem is not whether the socialist countries and forces will or will not support a war which breaks out independently of them or is forced on them, but whether they should themselves make the decision whether war is or is not indispensable for the resolution of the existing contradictions, whether they are to pursue a policy of war or a policy of peace and coexistence.* There is only one solution to this dilemma which is in conformity with Marxism and the humanistic spirit of socialism: if there are any other ways of resolving these contradictions other than war, the socialists forces can and should pursue solely a policy of peace and coexistence. We all know not only that there are these other ways of solving the contradictions, but also that war as such simply is not an instrument capable of resolving such contradictions. . . .

If we leave aside certain accurate evaluations of colonial and revolutionary wars, the attitude of the Chinese theoreticians boils down to a theory that a just war is any war waged by a socialist country, because socialism is progressive and capitalism is reactionary. Here in fact the theory of just and unjust wars is brought to the ridiculous conclusion that any war which *I* wage is a just war.

However, if we put things in this way, the question of whether or not war is just loses any meaning whatsoever. Namely, if we have in mind a defensive war, it is out of place to attack the Yugoslavs, for in Yugoslavia there is really not a man who would not consider that socialism must defend itself if attacked. If however we think of the question of whether the socialist countries should strive for such a world war, once again the question of justness or unjustness is not evaluated from the standpoint of the real consequences of such a war for the peoples of the world, for the fate of socialism and social progress. Here in advance we must declare that such a war is in principle contrary to the interests of socialism and not even the Chinese interpretation of the theory about just and unjust wars can change anything here. . . .

When we take together all the Chinese theories which we have discussed and through which the Yugoslav policy of peaceable and active coexistence is criticised, we get the following chain of argument: coexistence is untenable, since war is inevitable as the form which the revolutionary resolution of contradictions in the "international class struggle" takes, while war in itself is just, so it is wrong to disseminate any illusions about peace and coexistence, but we should set a course for war, in which we would be the stronger, a war in which the sacrifices would "be redeemed" and which would terminate in the victory of socialism in the whole world. . . .

It is in complete opposition to the spirit of Marxism to take the fact that it is waged by a socialist country as the sole criterion of the "justness" of a war. In the last resort, it is not merely a matter of whether a war in the name of socialism, against capitalist countries, can under certain conditions—objectively, against the will of the socialist countries—turn out to be a war with the working-class of those countries, which will defend its own bourgeoisie in the name of national independence. What matters is that such a war might impose more backward political forms of socialism in much more developed social-economic circumstances, and in this way play a reactionary role. It is also possible in such a war for unsocialist trends, such as hegemonism and similar phenomena, to come to expression. And, finally, it is not difficult to deny the existence of socialism in another country and then "in the name of socialism" to declare "just" any pressure on that country, to the point of war itself against it.

Is such a possibility merely a theoretical supposition? No, we have a very recent example of it—the pressure on socialist Yugoslavia. All the Chinese authors without exception—in one form or another—deny the socialist character of Yugoslavia, and this, in the spirit of the logic of the Chinese views of the moment, means that they are declaring Yugoslavia to be an "outlaw" country. Precisely for this reason today even more than in the past those principles of Marx, Engels and Lenin by which they fundamentally condemned and rejected any policy aimed at the forcible imposition of socialism or of one or another set of socialist relationships from outside, by war, should be cherished. That attitude on the one hand makes for a realistic appraisal of the harmful immediate social-political consequences of the responsibility which the socialist forces would assume if they adopted war as an instrument for the imposition of socialism, and on the other hand just as realistic an understanding that no socialist country merely by being socialist automatically becomes immune to egoistic aims or acts. Everybody knows that distortions, errors and the emergence of all manner of negative trends not only go with the development of a young society on the socialist road, but may also appear in the foreign policy of a socialist country, especially in the relations between the nations in the period during which neither narrow-minded nationalism or great-state hegemonism are quite dead as notions. Precisely for this reason the classics of Marxism never excluded the possibility of a socialist country also waging *an unjust war*. Practice confirms that such phenomena are not quite out of the question. . . .

Were the Chinese theories to become the governing factor in socialist international policy, the very relations between the socialist countries would be condemned to fundamental deformation. Practice in the example of Yugoslavia shows that this has already happened once in history, and in no small way—in the period of the Stalinist pressure on Yugoslavia—and that it is now precisely the leadership of the Communist Party of China that is making an effort once again to introduce and "further develop" this policy of pressure on the internal socialist development of Yugoslavia and on Yugoslavia's international policy. For this attitude of theirs the Chinese theoreticians make little effort to find many reasons, theoretical or ideological.

At least since Marx we have known the characteristics which define the socialist character of a country. But the Chinese theoreticians have found a simpler formula: any country which is not formally in the organisation known as the socialist camp is a capitalist country. Thereby Yugoslavia is automatically classed with the countries to which what anybody pleases may be done, all in the name of "socialism" and "Marxism." As the Chinese propagandists say, "a struggle to the very end must be waged against Yugoslav revisionism." What is the meaning of those words "to the very end?" It can mean nothing else but that a socialist country which does not endorse Chinese views and demands can be settled with by force. . . . This certainly throws a light "to the very end" on the Chinese theory of what constitutes just and what unjust war.

— 17 —

CAN A SOCIALIST COUNTRY WAGE AN "UNJUST WAR"? LATEST REVELATIONS OF A REVISIONIST

September 2, 1960*

Borba has carried chapters from a new book by Edvard Kardelj, which bears the pretentious title "Socialism and War." . . .

Kardelj has this time chosen a polemic with the Chinese Communist as the occasion for propagandizing his revisionist ideas. . . .

With this new book Kardelj comes to the aid of those who are inspiring the anti-Communist campaign. This book represents a revisionist attempt, on the pretense of combating "leftism" to drag into the workers' movement views that only the adversaries of communism will applaud. . . .

Kardelj's basic theoretical transgression is that in ana-

* A. Arguananryan and V. Korionov, *Pravda*, September 2, 1960, as translated by *Current Digest of the Soviet Press*, Vol. XII, No. 35. Reprinted by permission.

lyzing the problems of war he fails to establish the connection between wars and the struggle of the classes, to deal with war as an extension of politics by forcible means. Has war been historically inevitable? "Speaking abstractly," says Kardelj in answer to this question, "the inevitability of war has never been absolute, fatal. It has always depended on the correlation of forces." Kardelj's departure from Marxist-Leninist theories on the question of war is already visible in this answer.

Marxism-Leninism proceeds from the premise that war is an extension of politics by other, i.e., forcible, means. War is a historical category. It is linked with the antagonistic contradictions of classes and states. Wars, therefore, are the inevitable concomitant to all exploiter formations. . . .

Kardelj looks at this problem in another way. Failing to see the unavoidable connection between war and classes and class struggle, Kardelj claims that the issues of war and peace have always been settled by the correlation of forces. "War is inevitable," he writes, "if the forces of peace are too weak to prevent its outbreak. War may be done away with if the forces of peace prove mightier than the forces of war."

Kardelj even alleges that Marx and Engels did not link the possibility of preventing war with the transition to socialism. He maintains that the founders of scientific communism, foreseeing a time when war would cease to be inevitable and the possibility that this would happen "did not link them with any specific dates in history but merely with the maturation of a number of facts of social development, material and ideological—political alike, that would condition people's actions."

And yet, Marx, Engels and Lenin always proceeded from the premise that under the domination of capitalism as well as of the preceding exploiter formations, war was inevitable. With capitalism exercising sway all over the globe no changes in the correlation of the forces of war and peace can do away with war. The elimination of wars was linked by the founders of Marxism-Leninism with the abolition of antagonistic classes and the establishment of socialism.

E. Kardelj infers the inevitability of wars from the correlation of forces, studiously avoiding the question of

what correlation of forces is involved and in what da
The correlation of forces in the day when capitalism w
the sole world system was one thing. Quite another is th
correlation of forces at a time when the world has sp
into two systems, and alongside the moribund systems
imperialism has appeared the new world system of s
cialism, full of strength and confidently on the wa
up. . . .

Why does Kardelj stubbornly sidestep the point tha
only with the advent and consolidation of the world sc
cialist system has the prevention of war become a realist
possibility? There is a purpose behind this. The thin
is that according to Kardelj war is latent not only in th
nature of imperialism but in the nature of the sociali
countries as well.

Kardelj's breach with Marxism-Leninism becomes e
pecially distinct on this question. There the mask final
drops off the revisionist and he appears in his true guise.

The facts of life are flatly against Kardelj. He is there
fore constrained to mention that "socialism (to the e
tent that genuinely Socialist social relations are involve
and not elements of the old in the new) not only ca
not be a source of war, but its consolidation in the worl
has to become a factor in lessening the danger of wa
and eliminating the inevitability of war." But Karde
accompanies even this forced acknowledgment with a
sorts of qualifications great and small, with his effort t
sow doubts as to the "genuineness of socialist social re
lations" and his obscure reference to elements of the ol
in the new. Kardelj needs these qualifications to unde
mine the people's trust in socialism, in which they see
mighty source of peace.

The apostle of Yugoslav revisionism brashly assert
that the founders of Marxism did not look upon the vic
tory of socialism in a country as an absolute obstac
to war.

This is monstrous, but a fact. Kardelj assumes that
socialist state may be the bearer of an aggressive wa
Thus, having started from the figment of "socialist hege
monism," from the claim that the ambition to dominat
other countries is inherent in the "socialist bloc" as we
as the imperialist, the Yugoslav revisionists have no
ended up at a logical point. They place responsibility i

advance on the socialist state for the possible unleashing of war. . . .

He conditions the preservation of peace upon all sorts of typical revisionist "ifs." He proclaims that "no one socialist state automatically becomes immune to antagonistic tendencies and actions just because it is socialist." Kardelj tries to argue that "the classical writers of Marxism did not rule out the possibility that a socialist country might wage an unjust war."

Needless to say, Kardelj does not adduce a single fact to bear out his figments, for the single reason that such facts are non-existent. But all the same the revisionist has done his work. He has supplied reactionary bourgeois propagandists with one more "agreement" in their anti-Communist slander.

It should be said that altogether Kardelj's attitude to socialism and to socialist gains that the people have scored at the cost of the greatest sacrifice and suffering is more than strange. Time and time again in his writings the tangent creeps in that socialism too has inherent negative traits—hegemonism, a tendency to reactionary wars, etc. Surely this is attested to by the author's profuse and grandiloquent statements that the fact that a certain war is being waged by a socialist country is not the sole criterion of the "justice" of that war. Yes, he actually encloses the word justice in quotation marks. What is more, he says that "such a war may impose backward political forms of socialism in socio-economic conditions that are considerably more developed, and objectively play a reactionary role. It is also possible that in the course of such a war non-socialist tendencies may manifest themselves along with hegemonism and other similar phenomena."

What need had Kardelj of these arguments? After all, he is of course well aware that Marxism-Leninism has always most emphatically disavowed and still disavows the "export" of revolution. Is it not to bolster the imperialist thesis on the export of revolution that Kardelj is disseminating his point of view? That is not all. Kardelj is trying to put into circulation yet another accusation against the socialist countries: the possibility that one socialist country may forcibly impose its forms of development on another socialist country. It is no coincidence that he should refer to the possibility "even of antagonistic contradictions" between socialist states. . . .

The revisionists, and in the first place the Yugoslav revisionists, have long since foresaken the Marxist analysis of the radical distinction, the extremely profound contradictions between the world socialist system and the world capitalist system. Repudiation of the class approach to the fundamental questions of foreign policy has brought the Belgrade theorists to a point where they pretend not to notice the existence of a socialist camp that consistently upholds the peace, freedom and progress of nations and of an imperialist camp that is preparing a world thermonuclear catastrophe. For the reformist there is no difference between the socialist international policy of the working class and the anti-popular policy of the financial and industrial oligarchy.

One might think that this kind of thing represents the position that is usual for revisionists. The facts argue, however, that this notorious stand "outside of blocs" is more and more clearly assuming the nature of a link with definite circles in the aggressive imperialist bloc. The appearance of Kardelj's new book lends yet another highly significant touch to this political line. The people in Belgrade no longer limit themselves to calumny against the socialist countries. The Belgrade theorists are now trying to impugn the peace-loving character of the socialist camp's foreign policy. Communists in all countries and the millions of people who are selflessly fighting for peace now know that the latest piece of slander against socialism bears the plainly visible stamp "Made in Yugoslavia." . . .

Part VI

The Unity of Opposites: The 1960 Conference of 81 Communist Parties

In the main, the 81 Communist Parties Conference succeeded in achieving its major purpose: the resolution of the theoretical dispute between Communist China and the Soviet Union.

On the old issues of war, peaceful coexistence, and the nature of the transition to Socialism in non-Communist countries, the Soviet view prevailed.

If the Chinese obtained a number of concessions, these related to areas where Soviet policy during 1960 had indicated a willingness to compromise.

The sections of the Declaration defining in a new way the position of the Soviet Union in the Socialist camp, the more active support promised to wars of national liberation, and the harsher condemnation of Yugoslav Revisionism represented a partial victory for the Chinese.

Nevertheless, the 81 Party statement is replete with qualifications that would allow the Soviet Union as well as the Chinese to interpret the document according to their own preferences. As the Yugoslavs took pains to point out, Soviet and Chinese commentaries on the November Conference that were prepared for domestic consumption continued to reflect national views and policies.

— 18 —

STATEMENT ISSUED BY THE CONFERENCE OF REPRESENTATIVES OF COMMUNIST PARTIES

Moscow—November, 1960*

. . . The People's Democratic Republics of Albania, Bulgaria, Hungary, the German Democratic Republic, the Democratic Republic of Vietnam, China, the Korean People's Democratic Republic, Mongolia, Poland, Rumania and the Czechoslovak Socialist Republic, which, together with the great Soviet Union, form the mighty socialist camp, have within a historically short period made remarkable progress in socialist construction. . . .

The socialist countries and the socialist camp as a whole owe their achievements to the proper application of the general objective laws governing socialist construction, with due regard to the historical peculiarities of each country and to the interests of the entire socialist system. They owe them to the efforts of the peoples of those countries, to their close fraternal cooperation and mutual internationalist assistance from the Soviet Union.

The experience of development of the socialist countries is added evidence that mutual assistance and support, and utilization of all the advantages of unity and solidarity among the countries of the socialist camp, are a primary international condition for their achievements and suc-

* New York *Times,* December 7, 1960. Reprinted by permission.

cesses. Imperialist, renegade and revisionist hopes of a split within the socialist camp are built on sand and doomed to failure. All the socialist countries cherish the unity of the socialist camp like the apple of their eye.

The world economic system of socialism is united by common socialist relations of production and is developing in accordance with the economic laws of socialism. . . .

It requires study of collective experience, extended cooperation and fraternal mutual assistance, gradual elimination, along these lines, of historical differences in the levels of economic development, and the provision of a material basis for a more or less simultaneous transition of all the peoples of the socialist system to communism.

Socialist construction in the various countries is a source of collective experience for the socialist camp as a whole. A thorough study of this experience by the fraternal parties, and its proper utilization and elaboration with due regard to specific conditions and national peculiarities are an immutable law of the development of every socialist country. . . . The socialist camp is a social, economic and political community of free and sovereign peoples united by the close bonds of international socialist solidarity, by common interests and objectives, and following the path of socialism and communism. It is an inviolable law of the mutual relations between socialist countries strictly to adhere to the principles of Marxism-Leninism and socialist internationalism. Every country in the socialist camp is insured genuinely equal rights and independence. Guided by the principles of complete equality, mutual advantage and comradely mutual assistance, the socialist states improve their all-round economic, political and cultural cooperation, which meets both the interests of each socialist country and those of the socialist camp as a whole.

One of the greatest achievements of the world socialist system is the practical confirmation of the Marxist-Leninist thesis that national antagonisms diminish with the decline of class antagonisms.

In contrast to the laws of the capitalist system, which is characterized by antagonistic contradictions between classes, nations and states leading to armed conflicts, there are no objective causes in the nature of the socialist system for contradictions and conflicts between the peoples and states belonging to it. Its development leads to greater unity among the states and nations and to the consolidation of all the forms of cooperation between them.

Under socialism, the development of national economy, culture and statehood goes hand in hand with the strengthening and development of the entire world socialist system, and with an ever greater consolidation of the unity of nations. The interests of the socialist system as a whole and national interests are harmoniously combined. It is on this basis that the moral and political unity of all the peoples of the great socialist community has arisen and has been growing. Fraternal friendship and mutual assistance of peoples, born of the socialist system, have superseded the political isolation and national egoism typical of capitalism.

The common interests of the peoples of the socialist countries and the interests of peace and socialism demand the proper combination of the principles of socialist internationalism and socialist patriotism in politics. Every Communist party which has become the ruling party in the state, bears historical responsibility for the destinies of both its country and the entire socialist camp.

The declaration of 1957 points out quite correctly that undue emphasis on the role of national peculiarities and departure from the universal truth of Marxism-Leninism regarding the socialist revolution and socialist construction prejudice the common cause of socialism.

The declaration also states quite correctly that Marxism-Leninism demands creative application of the general principles of socialist revolution and socialist construction, depending on the specific historical conditions in the country concerned, and does not permit of a mechanical copying of the policies and tactics of the Communist parties of other countries. Disregard of national peculiarities may lead to the party of the proletariat being isolated from reality, from the masses, and may injure the socialist cause.

Manifestations of nationalism and national narrow-mindedness do not disappear automatically with the establishment of the socialist system. If fraternal relations and friendship between the socialist countries are to be strengthened, it is necessary that the Communist and workers parties pursue a Marxist-Leninist internationalist policy, that all working people be educated in a spirit of internationalism and patriotism, and that a resolute struggle be waged to eliminate the survivals of bourgeois nationalism and chauvinism. . . .

The time has come when the socialist states have, by forming a world system, become an international force exerting a powerful influence on world development. There are now real opportunities of solving cardinal problems of modern times in a new way, in the interests of peace, democracy and socialism.

The problem of war and peace is the most burning problem of our time.

War is a constant companion of capitalism. The system of exploitation of man by man and the system of extermination of man by man are two aspects of the capitalist system. Imperialism has already inflicted two devastating world wars on mankind and now threatens to plunge it into an even more terrible catastrophe.

Monstrous means of mass annihilation and destruction have been developed which, if used in a new war, can cause unheard-of destruction to entire countries and reduce key centers of world industry and culture to ruins. Such a war would bring death and suffering to hundreds of millions of people, among them people in countries not involved in it. Imperialism spells grave danger to the whole of mankind.

The peoples must now be more vigilant than ever. As long as imperialism exists there will be soil for wars of aggression.

The peoples of all countries know that the danger of a new world war still persists. U.S. imperialism is the main force of aggression and war. Its policy embodies the ideology of militant reaction.

The U.S. imperialists, together with the imperialists of Britain, France and West Germany, have drawn many countries into NATO, CENTO, SEATO and other military blocs. Under the guise of combating the "Communist menace," it has enmeshed the so-called "free world," that is, capitalist countries which depend on them, in a net-

work of military bases spearheaded first and foremost
against the socialist countries.

The existence of these blocs and bases endangers universal peace and security and not only encroaches upon
the sovereignty but also imperils the very life of those
countries which put their territory at the disposal of the
U.S. militarists. . . .

The aggressive nature of imperialism has not changed.
But real forces have appeared that are capable of foiling
its plans of aggression. War is not fatally inevitable. Had
the imperialists been able to do what they wanted, they
would already have plunged mankind into the abyss of
the calamities and horrors of a new world war.

But the time is past when the imperialists could decide
at will whether there should or should not be war. More
than once in the past years the imperialists have brought
mankind to the brink of world catastrophe by starting
local wars. . . .

The time has come when the attempts of the imperialist
aggressors to start a world war can be curbed. World war
can be prevented by the joint efforts of the world socialist
camp, the international working class, the national-liberation movement, all the countries opposing war and all
peace-loving forces.

The development of international relations in our day
is determined by the struggle of the two social systems—
the struggle of the forces of socialism, peace and democracy against the forces of imperialism, reaction and aggression—a struggle in which the superiority of the forces
of socialism, peace and democracy is becoming increasingly obvious.

For the first time in history, war is opposed by great
and organized forces: the mighty Soviet Union, which
now leads the world in the decisive branches of science
and technology, the entire socialist camp, which has
placed its great material and political might at the serv-
ice of peace, a growing number of peace-loving countries
of Asia, Africa and Latin America, which have a vital
interest in preserving peace, the international working
class and its organizations, above all the Communist
parties, the national-liberation movement of the peoples
of the colonies and dependent countries, the world peace
movement, and the neutral countries which want no share

in the imperialist policy of war and advocate peaceful co-existence.

The policy of peaceful coexistence is also favored by a definite section of the bourgeoisie of the developed capitalist countries, which takes a sober view of the relationship of forces and of the dire consequences of a modern war. The broadest possible united front of peace supporters, fighters against the imperialist policy of aggression and war inspired by U.S. imperialism, is essential to preserve world peace. Concerted and vigorous actions of all the forces of peace can safeguard the peace and prevent a new war.

The democratic and peace forces today have no task more pressing than that of safeguarding humanity against a global thermonucleur disaster. The unprecedented destructive power of modern means of warfare demands that the main actions of the anti-war and peace-loving forces be directed towards preventing war. The struggle against war cannot be put off until war breaks out, for then it may prove too late for many areas of the globe and for their population to combat it. . . .

The Communist parties regard the fight for peace as their prime task. They call on the working class, trade unions, cooperatives, women's and youth leagues and organizations, on all working people, irrespective of their political and religious convictions, firmly to repulse by mass struggles all acts of aggression on the part of the imperialists.

But should the imperialist maniacs start war, the peoples will sweep capitalism out of existence and bury it. . . .

The near future will bring the forces of peace and socialism new successes. The U.S.S.R. will become the leading industrial power of the world. China will become a mighty industrial state. The socialist system will be turning out more than half the world industrial product. The peace zone will expand. The working-class movement in the capitalist countries and the national-liberation movement in the colonies and dependencies will achieve new victories. The disintegration of the colonial system will become completed. The superiority of the forces of socialism and peace will be absolute.

In these conditions a real possibility will have arisen

to exclude world war from the life of a society even before socialism achieves complete victory on earth, with capitalism still existing in a part of the world. . . .

. . . Peace is a loyal ally of socialism, for time is working for socialism against capitalism.

The policy of peaceful coexistence is a policy of mobilizing the masses and launching vigorous action against the enemies of peace. Peaceful coexistence of states does not imply renunciation of the class struggle, as the revisionists claim. The coexistence of states with different social systems is a form of class struggle between socialism and capitalism.

In conditions of peaceful coexistence favorable opportunities are provided for the development of the class struggle in the capitalist countries and the national-liberation movement of the peoples of the colonial and dependent countries. In their turn, the successes of the revolutionary class and national-liberation struggle promote peaceful coexistence.

The Communists consider it their duty to fortify the faith of the people in the possibility of furthering peaceful coexistence, their determination to prevent world war. They will do their utmost for the people to weaken imperialism and limit its sphere of action by an active struggle for peace, democracy and national liberation.

Peaceful coexistence of countries with different social systems does not mean conciliation of the socialist and bourgeois ideologies. On the contrary, it implies intensification of the struggle of the working class, of all the Communist parties, for the triumph of socialist ideas. But ideological and political disputes between states must not be settled through war. . . .

The choice of social system is the inalienable right of the people of each country. Socialist revolution is not an item of import and cannot be imposed from without. It is a result of the internal development of the country concerned, of the utmost sharpening of social contradictions in it.

The Communist parties, which guide themselves by the Marxist-Leninist doctrine, have always been against the export of revolution. At the same time, they fight resolutely against imperialist export of counter-revolution. They consider it their internationalist duty to call on the peoples of all countries to unite, to rally all their internal forces, to act vigorously and, relying on the might of the world Socialist system, to prevent or firmly resist imperialist interference in the affairs of any people who have risen in revolution.

The Marxist-Leninist parties head the struggle of the working class, the masses of working people, for the accomplishment of the Socialist revolution and the establishment of the dictatorship of the proletariat in one form or another. The forms and course of development of the Socialist revolution will depend on the specific balance of the class forces in the country concerned, on the organization and maturity of the working class and its vanguard, and on the extent of the resistance put up by the ruling classes.

Whatever form of dictatorship of the proletariat is established, it will always signify an extension of democracy, a transition from formal, bourgeois democracy to genuine democracy, to democracy for working people.

The Communist parties reaffirm the propositions put forward by the declaration of 1957 with regard to the forms of transition of different countries from capitalism to socialism.

The declaration points out that the working class and its vanguard—the Marxist-Leninist party—seek to achieve the Socialist revolution by peaceful means. This would accord with the interests of the working class and the people as a whole, with the national interests of the country.

Today in a number of capitalist countries the working class, headed by its vanguard, has the opportunity, given a united working-class and popular front or other workable forms of agreement and political cooperation between the different parties and public organizations, to unite a majority of the people, win state power without civil war and insure the transfer of the basic means of production to the hands of the people.

Relying on the majority of the people and resolutely rebuffing the opportunist elements incapable of relinquishing the policy of compromise with the capitalists and landlords, the working class can defeat the reactionary, anti-popular forces, secure a firm majority in parliament, transform parliament from an instrument serving the class

interests of the bourgeoisie into an instrument serving the
working people, launch an extra-parliamentary mass
struggle, smash the resistance of the reactionary forces
and create the necessary conditions for peaceful realization of the Socialist revolution.

All this will be possible only by broad and ceaseless
development of the class struggle of the workers, peasant
masses and the urban middle strata against big monopoly
capital, against reaction, for profound social reforms, for
peace and socialism.

In the event of the exploiting classes' resorting to violence against people, the possibility of non-peaceful
transition to socialism should be borne in mind. Leninism
teaches, and experience confirms, that the ruling classes
never relinquish power voluntarily. In this case the degree
of bitterness and the forms of the class struggle will depend not so much on the proletariat as on the resistance
put up by the reactionary circles to the will of the overwhelming majority of the people, on these circles using
force at one or another stage of the struggle for socialism.

The actual possibility of the one or the other way of
transition to socialism in each individual country depends
on the concrete historical conditions.

In our time, when communism is not only the most advanced doctrine but an actually existing social system
which has proved its superiority over capitalism, conditions are particularly favorable for expanding the influence of the Communist parties, vigorously exposing
anti-communism, a slogan under which the capitalist
class wages its struggle against the proletariat, and winning the broadest sections of the working masses for
Communist ideas. . . .

The growth of the Communist parties and their organizational consolidation, the victories of the Communist
parties in a number of countries in the struggle against
deviation, elimination of the harmful consequences of
the personality cult, the greater influence of the world
Communist movement open new prospects for the successful accomplishment of the tasks facing the Communist parties.

Marxist-Leninist parties regard it as an inviolable law
of their activity steadfastly to observe the Leninist standards of party life in keeping with the principle of demo-

cratic centralism. They consider that they must cherish party unity like the apple of their eye, strictly to adhere to the principle of party democracy and collective leadership, for they attach, in keeping with the organizational principles of Leninism, great importance to the role of the leading party bodies in the life of the party, to work indefatigably for the strengthening of their bonds with the party membership and with the broad masses of the working people, not to allow the personality cult, which shackles creative thought and initiative of Communists, vigorously to promote the activity of Communist, and to encourage criticism and self-criticism in their ranks.

The Communist parties have ideologically defeated the revisionists in their ranks who sought to divert them from the Marxist-Leninist path. Each Communist Party and the international Communist movement as a whole have become still stronger, ideologically and organizationally, in the struggle against revisionism, Right-wing opportunism.

The Communist parties have unanimously condemned the Yugoslav variety of international opportunism, a variety of modern revisionist theories in concentrated form. After betraying Marxism-Leninism, which they termed obsolete, the leaders of the League of Communists of Yugoslavia opposed their anti-Leninist revisionist program to the declaration of 1957, they set the League of Communists of Yugoslavia against the international Communist movement as a whole, severed their country from the Socialist camp, made it dependent on so-called aid from United States and other imperialists, and thereby exposed the Yugoslav people to the danger of losing the revolutionary gains achieved through a heroic struggle.

The Yugoslav revisionists carry on subversive work against the Socialist camp and the world Communist movement. Under the pretext of an extra-bloc policy, they engage in activities which prejudice the unity of all the peace-loving forces and countries. Further exposure of the leaders of the Yugoslav revisionists, and active struggle to safeguard the Communist movement and the working-class movement from the anti-Leninist ideas of the Yugoslav revisionists, remains an essential task of the Marxist-Leninist parties.

The practical struggles of the working class and the

entire course of social development have furnished a brilliant new proof of the great all-conquering power and vitality of Marxism-Leninism, and have thoroughly refuted all modern revisionist theories.

The further development of the Communist and working-class movement calls, as stated in the Moscow declaration of 1957, for continuing a determined struggle on two fronts—against revisionism, which remains the main danger, and against dogmatism and sectarianism.

Revisionism, Right-wing opportunism, which mirrors the bourgeois ideology in theory and practice, distorts Marxism-Leninism, emasculates its revolutionary essence and thereby paralyzes the revolutionary will of the working class, disarms and demobilizes the workers, the masses of the working people, in their struggle against oppression by imperialists and exploiters, for peace, democracy and national liberation, for the triumph of socialism.

Dogmatism and sectarianism in theory and practice can also become the main danger at some stage of development of individual parties, unless combated unrelentingly.

They rob revolutionary parties of the ability to develop Marxism-Leninism through scientific analysis and apply it creatively according to the specific conditions, they isolate Communists from the broad masses of the working people, doom them to passive expectation or Leftist, adventurist actions in the revolutionary struggle, prevent them from making a timely and correct estimate of the changing situation and of new experience, using all opportunities to bring about the victory of the working class and all democratic forces in the struggle against imperialism, reaction and war danger, and thereby prevent the peoples from achieving victory in their just struggle.

At a time when imperialist reaction is joining forces to fight communism, it is particularly imperative vigorously to consolidate the world Communist movement. Unity and solidarity redouble the strength of our movement and provide a reliable guarantee that the great cause of communism will make victorious progress and all enemy attacks will be effectively repelled.

Communists throughout the world are united by the great doctrine of Marxism-Leninism and by a joint struggle for its realization. The interests of the Communist movement require solidarity in adherence by every Communist party to the estimates and conclusions concerning the common tasks in the struggle against imperialism, for peace, democracy and socialism, jointly reached by the fraternal parties at their meetings.

The interest of the struggle for the working-class cause demand ever closer unity of the ranks of each Communist party and of the great army of Communists of all countries, they demand of them unity of will and action. It is the supreme internationalist duty of every Marxist-Leninist party to work continuously for greater unity in the world Communist movement.

A resolute defense of the unity of the world Communist movement on the principles of Marxism-Leninism and proletarian internationalism, and the prevention of any actions which may undermine that unity, are a necessary condition for victory in the struggle for national independence, democracy and peace, for the successful accomplishment of the tasks of the Socialist revolution and of the building of socialism and communism. Violation of these principles would impair the forces of communism.

All the Marxist-Leninist parties are independent and have equal rights, they shape their policies according to the specific conditions in their respective countries and in keeping with Marxist-Leninist principles, and support each other. The success of the working-class cause in any country is unthinkable without the internationalist solidarity of all Marxist-Leninist parties. Every party is responsible to the working class, to the working people of its country, to the international working-class and Communist movement as a whole.

The Communist and workers parties hold meetings whenever necessary to discuss urgent problems, to exchange experience, acquaint themselves with each other's views and positions, work out common views through consultations and coordinate joint actions in the struggle for common goals.

Whenever a party wants to clear up questions relating to the activities of another fraternal party, its leadership approaches the leadership of the party concerned. If necessary, they hold meetings and consultations.

The experience and results of the meetings of representatives of the Communist parties held in recent years, particularly the results of the two major meetings—that of November, 1957, and this meeting—show that in present-day conditions such meetings are an effective form of exchanging views and experience, enriching Marxist-Leninist theory by collective effort and elaborating a common attitude in the struggle for common objectives.

The Communist and workers parties unanimously declare that the Communist party of the Soviet Union has been, and remains, the universally recognized vanguard of the world Communist movement, being the most experienced and steeled contingent of the international Communist movement. The experience which the Communist party of the Soviet Union has gained in the struggle for the victory of the working class, in Socialist construction and in the full-scale construction of communism, is of fundamental significance for the whole of the world Communist movement.

The example of the Soviet Communist party and its fraternal solidarity inspire all the Communist parties in their struggle for peace and socialism, and represent the revolutionary principles of proletarian internationalism applied in practice.

The historic decisions of the Twentieth Congress of the Soviet Communist party are not only of great importance for the Soviet Communist party and Communist construction in the U.S.S.R., but have initiated a new stage in the world Communist movement, and have promoted its development on the basis of Marxism-Leninism.

All Communist and workers parties contribute to the development of the great theory of Marxism-Leninism. Mutual assistance and support in relations between all the fraternal Marxist-Leninist parties embody the revolutionary principles of proletarian internationalism applied in practice. . . .

— 19 —

KHRUSHCHEV'S REVIEW OF THE 81-PARTY COMMUNIST CONFERENCE

January, 1961*

. . . Comrades, the struggle between the Communist and all the people's forces, on the one hand, and the forces of imperialism, on the other, is entering a new stage. In these conditions the solidarity of the socialist camp and of the entire international Communist movement acquires paramount importance. Our solidarity on the principles of Marxism-Leninism, of proletarian internationalism, is the main condition for the victory of the working class over imperialism. We hold sacred the great Lenin's behest to march forward shoulder to shoulder. The unity of our ranks multiplies the forces of Communism tenfold. Solidarity, solidarity and once again solidarity—this is the law of the international Communist movement.

It follows from the very essence of Leninism that each Marxist-Leninist party must not permit, either in its own ranks or in the international Communist movement, any actions that might undermine its unity and solidarity. . . .

It should be noted that the delegation of the Communist Party of the Soviet Union set forth at the conference its point of view concerning the formula that the Soviet Union stands at the head of the socialist camp and the C.P.S.U. at the head of the Communist movement. Our delegation stated that we viewed this formula above all as high appreciation of the services of our party, founded by Lenin, and expressed its deep gratitude to all the fraternal parties. Our party, reared by Lenin, has always considered it its primary duty to fulfill its interna-

---

* The Current Digest of the Soviet Press, Vol. XIII, No. 4. Reprinted by permission.

tionalist obligations to the international working class. The delegation assured the conference participants that our party would continue to carry high the banner of proletarian internationalism and would spare no effort to fulfill its internationalist obligations.

At the same time, the delegation of the C.P.S.U. proposed that this formula not be included in the Statement or other documents of the Communist movement.

As for the principles of relations among the fraternal parties, the C.P.S.U. very definitely expressed its position on this question at the 21st Party Congress. From the rostrum of the Congress we declared to the whole world that in the Communist movement, as in the socialist camp, there has been and is full equality and solidarity of all the Communist and Workers' Parties and the socialist countries. In reality the Communist Party of the Soviet Union does not lead other parties. There are no "superior" and "subordinate" parties in the Communist movement. All the Communist Parties are equal and independent, and all bear responsibility for the destiny of the Communist movement, for its victories and failures. Each Communist and Workers' Party is responsible to the working class, to the working people of its country and to the entire international workers' and Communist movement.

The role of the Soviet Union does not lie in its leading the other socialist countries, but in having been first to pave the way to socialism, in being the most powerful country in the world socialist system, in having accumulated great positive experience in the struggle to build socialism and in having been first to enter the period of full-scale building of communism. The Statement stresses that the Communist Party of the Soviet Union, as the most experienced and steeled detachment of the international Communist movement, has been and continues to be the universally recognized vanguard of the world Communist movement.

Today, when there is a large group of socialist countries, each facing its own tasks, when there are 87 Communist and Workers' Parties, each of them also facing its own tasks, it is impossible to lead the socialist countries and the Communist Parties from any center. It is impos-

sible and, furthermore, not necessary. The Communist
Parties have developed tempered Marxist-Leninist cadres,
capable of leading their own parties and their own countries.

Furthermore, in actual fact, as is well known, the
C.P.S.U. does not issue directives to any other parties.
The fact that we will be called "the head" is of no advantage either for our party or for other parties. On the contrary, it only creates difficulties.

As evident from the text of the Statement, the fraternal
parties agreed with the reasoning of our delegation. The
question might arise: Will not our international solidarity
be weakened by the fact that this proposition is not written down in the Statement? No, it will not. At present
there are no statutes regulating relations among the
parties, but we do have a common Marxist-Leninist
ideology, and loyalty to it is the main condition of our
solidarity and unity. It is necessary to be guided consistently by the teaching of Marx, Engels and Lenin, persistently to put into practice the principles of Marxism-
Leninism, and then the internationalist solidarity of the
Communist movement will constantly increase. . . .

Today, when the socialist countries, guided by this
teaching, are achieving major successes in the economic
competition with the capitalist states, the broad masses of
the people see that socialism, communism, is the greatest
force of our time and that the future belongs to communism.

Of course in the process of building socialism and communism new forms and methods emerge which yield good
results in the achievement of great socialist aims. Since
different conditions exist in the different socialist countries, it is natural that each Communist Party applies
Marxist-Leninist theory in accordance with the conditions
in its country. Therefore we must treat with understanding this kind of aspiration of the fraternal parties, who
know best the conditions and features of their countries. . . .

But of course one must not inflate the importance of
these features, exaggerate them and fail to see the main
general path of socialist construction charted by the
teaching of Marx and Lenin. We have always firmly defended and will continue to defend the purity of the great

teaching of Marxism-Leninism and the basic principle
for putting it into practice.

The representatives of the Communist and Worker
Parties exchanged views on questions of the present-da
international situation and discussed pressing problems o
the Communist and workers' movement, or, as the com
rades put it figuratively at the conference, "we set ou
watches." Indeed, the socialist countries and the Com
munist Parties need to set their watches. When someone
watch runs fast or slow, it is adjusted so that it runs pro
erly. So in the Communist movement, too, it is nece
sary to set our watches so that our mighty army will kee
in step and march with confident stride toward com
munism. If I might put it figuratively, Marxism-Leninis
and the jointly drafted documents of international Com
munist conferences are our tower clock.

Now that all the Communist and Workers' Parties ha
unanimously worked out decisions, each party w
sacredly and strictly abide by these decisions in al
activity. . . .

The Communist Party of the Soviet Union is firm
resolved to strengthen unity and friendship with all t
fraternal parties of the socialist countries, with the Mar
ist-Leninist parties of the whole world. In this connecti
I would like to speak of our invariable striving
strengthen ties of fraternal friendship with the Chine
Communist Party and with the great Chinese people.
its relations with the Chinese Communist Party our pa
is always guided by the premise that the friendship of t
two great peoples and the solidarity of our two parties
the largest in the international Communist movement
are of exceptional importance in the struggle for t
triumph of our common cause. Our party has alwa
exerted and will continue to exert every effort
strengthen this great friendship. We have one comm
goal with People's China and the Chinese Communists,
with the Communists of all countries—to safeguard pea
and build communism: common interests—the happin
and well-being of people of labor; and a firm comm
basis of principle—Marxism-Leninism.

The Communist Party of the Soviet Union and the S
viet people will do everything to make the unity of o
parties and our peoples increasingly strong, so as

only to disappoint our enemies but to shake them even more by our unity and to achieve our great goal—the triumph of communism. . . .

— 20 —

CHINESE COMMUNIST PARTY RESOLUTION ON THE MOSCOW MEETING

January, 1961*

Following is the resolution adopted by the 9th plenary session of the 8th Central Committee of the Communist Party of China on the meeting of representatives of Communist and Workers' Parties on January 18, 1961:

. . . The achievements of this meeting have greatly inspired the people of the world, who are striving for world peace, national liberation, democracy and socialism, have dealt heavy blows at the imperialists headed by the United States of America, the reactionaries of all countries and the Yugoslav revisionist clique, and have strengthened the solidarity of the socialist camp and the international communist movement on the new basis. . . . The Communist Party of China, always unswervingly upholding Marxism-Leninism and the principle of proletarian internationalism, will defend the statement of this meeting, just as it has defended the Moscow Declaration of 1957, and will resolutely strive for the realization of the common tasks set forth by this document. . . .

With the peoples of the world persevering in a resolute struggle against the forces of reaction and aggression headed by the United States, the peace, national-liberation, democratic and socialist movements are sure to win

* *Current Background*, No. 644, Hong Kong.

ever greater victories. Revolution is the affair of the peoples themselves in the various countries. The communists have always been against the export of revolution. They also resolutely oppose imperialist export of counter-revolution, against imperialist interference in the internal affairs of the people of various countries who have risen in revolution. The Communist Party of China and the Chinese people will, as in the past, make unremitting efforts in close unity with the fraternal parties and the revolutionary peoples of various countries to further the cause of the peoples of the world against imperialism and for world peace, national-liberation, democracy and socialism. They deem it their internationalist obligation to support the struggles of oppressed nations and oppressed peoples against imperialism.

The defense of world peace, the realization of peaceful coexistence and peaceful competition among countries of different social systems and the prevention of the new world war which is now being planned by the imperialists constitute the most pressing tasks for the peoples of the world. The imperialists headed by the United States are stubbornly persisting in a "cold war" policy leading to the catastrophe of nuclear war, intensifying the arming of the militarist forces of West Germany and Japan and fanatically engaging in armaments expansion and war preparations. Facts have proved that the aggressive nature of imperialism has not changed. As long as imperialism exists there will be soil for wars of aggression. The danger is not yet over that imperialism will launch a new and unprecedentedly destructive world war. It is more imperative than ever that the peoples should be especially vigilant. However, owing to the fundamental change in the international balance of class forces, a new world war can be prevented by the joint efforts of the powerful forces of our era—the socialist camp, the international working class, the national-liberation movement and all peace-loving countries and peoples. Peace can be effectively safeguarded provided there is reliance on the struggle of the masses of the people and provided a broad united front is established and expanded against the policies of aggression and war of the imperialists headed by the United States. Marxist-Leninists have never held that the way to socialist revolution necessarily lies through wars between states. The socialist countries have always persisted in the policy of peaceful co-existence and peaceful competition with the capitalist countries, advocated the settlement of international disputes through negotiation, advocated disarmament, the banning of nuclear weapons, the disbandment of military blocs, the dismantling of military bases in foreign territory, and the prevention of the revival of the militarist forces in West Germany and Japan. The peace proposals put forward by the socialist countries, and first of all by the Soviet Union, have won warm endorsement and support from people the world over. The Communist Party and the people of China have always regarded the safeguarding of world peace, the realization of peaceful co-existence and the prevention of another world war as their most urgent tasks in the international struggle. . . .

The solidarity of the socialist camp and of the international communist movement is the most important guarantee for victory in the struggle of all peoples for world peace, national liberation, democracy and socialism. This great solidarity is forged by common ideals and the common cause and has been developed and consolidated in the common struggle against the common enemy. It is based on Marxism-Leninism and the principle of proletarian internationalism. The Communist Party of China, in accordance with the principle of proletarian internationalism, has consistently striven to safeguard this great solidarity.

The Socialist countries carry on political, economic and cultural cooperation in accordance with the principles of complete equality, mutual respect for independence and sovereignty, mutual non-interference in internal affairs, mutual benefit and comradely mutual assistance. The Communist Parties of all countries are independent and equal and at the same time, in the spirit of proletarian internationalism, they must adhere to the common stand on the struggle against imperialism and for peace, national liberation, democracy and socialism as jointly adopted at meetings of the fraternal parties and must unite as one and support each other in their common cause. The statement of this meeting pointed out that the Communist and Workers' Parties should hold meetings whenever necessary to discuss urgent problems, acquaint themselves with each other's views and positions, work out common views through consultations and coordinate joint actions in the struggle for common goals. This is entirely necessary for the strengthening of solidarity and for victory in the common cause.

The great Marxist-Leninist teachings are the unshakable ideological foundation of the solidarity of the socialist camp and the unity of the international communist movement. In order to safeguard the purity of Marxism-Leninism and its creative application and development, it is necessary firmly to combat revisionism which mirrors bourgeois ideology and departs from and betrays Marxism-Leninism, and especially to combat Yugoslav revisionism. Modern revisionism is still the main danger for the international communist movement. At the same time, the tendencies of dogmatism and sectarianism, which are divorced from reality and from the masses, must also be opposed. The plenary session of the Central Committee of the Communist Party of China held that it is of particular importance at present to continue to carry out the principle of integrating the universal truth of Marxism-Leninism with the specific practice of China's revolution and construction, and to raise the level of Marxism-Leninism of the cadres of the Party and the state.

The unity between China and the Soviet Union and between the Chinese and the Soviet Parties is of particularly great significance. In the international communist movement, the great Communist Party of the Soviet Union is the vanguard with the longest history and richest experience. The great Soviet Union is the most advanced and most powerful country in the socialist camp. The Communist Party of China has consistently striven to maintain and strengthen the unity between the Chinese and the Soviet Parties and between the two countries, holding that this is in the fundamental interests of the peoples of China and the Soviet Union and also of the peoples of the whole world. The imperialists will never succeed in their hopeless scheme to split the unity between the Chinese and the Soviet Parties and between the two countries.

A STEP BACKWARD
Veljko Vlahović*

The statement published at the beginning of December last year, after the Conference of Communist and Workers' Parties in Moscow, is a document to which its authors attribute great importance and whose publication is described as "a historic event of world-wide significance." At the plenary sessions of the central committees of individual communist parties which were held at the end of last year and at the beginning of this year it was pointed out that the statement represented one of the most important Marxist-Leninist documents and that it served as "a guide to action" in the future activity of communist parties, both within various countries and on a large front of the struggle for socialism.

It is necessary to point out that the LCY does not attach the same significance to this document, just as it did not attach such significance to the previous statements and declarations of a similar type. . . .

The question arises whether it is at all necessary to refer to that part of the statement which relates to socialist Yugoslavia in view of the fact that we have heard about similar attacks on so many occasions already, or read about them in the speeches and articles of individual leaders of East European countries, especially in the speeches and articles of the most authoritative officials of the People's Republic of China and Albania. . . .

Obviously, their purpose is to inflict damage on socialist Yugoslavia, to render the development of socialism more difficult for her, to offer support to reactionary forces in the struggle against socialism in Yugoslavia, to make the international position of Yugoslavia more difficult in order to exert pressure on Yugoslav communists in order that they give up their specific road to the construction of

* Belgrade, 1961.

socialism, namely their concept that contemporary socialism should seek more advanced forms of development
than those which have already been achieved. And this
means that the statement, by its attack on Yugoslavia,
harms socialism in general, giving direct support to anti-
socialist forces in our country and the world at large. By
those attacks against socialist Yugoslavia the principles
of internationalism and socialist solidarity are grossly
violated. . . .

ON THE INTERPRETERS AND INTERPRETATIONS OF MARXISM

The entire practice of the development of socialism following the Second World War raises the question of discovering such forms of cooperation in the labour movement which would render impossible the application of
non-socialist methods and the non-socialist practices in
those relations.

In the decision on the dissolution of the Communist
International, as early as May 1943, it was stated
that . . .

"long before the war it became increasingly clear that if
the internal and international situation of individual countries became more complicated, the settlement of the tasks
facing the workers' movement of each country with the
forces of any international centre would be confronted
with insurmountable obstacles."

A whole series of examples from the past seventeen
years can be taken as a confirmation of this statement. In
the meantime the bureaucratic-dogmatic forces in the
labour movement made great efforts to establish such a
centre which would give appraisals and interpretations of
what is correct and what is incorrect, what is Marxian
and what is not Marxian. Such a situation has sharpened
the entire problem of the relations in the labour movement to an even greater extent, particularly the relations
between communist parties which are in power, and
created a suitable ground for various negative practices
and tendencies, especially the emergence of monopoly in
the labour movement.

The text of the statement issued by the Conference of
the communist and workers' parties in Moscow shows

that this problem was constantly present at the consultation. But, the fact is that it was not solved and moreover, the attitude taken towards socialist Yugoslavia as well as some other viewpoints indicate that the problem has been sharpened to an even greater extent.

It is obvious that the practice and the future development will mean a disappointment to all those who think that such consultations can become a kind of guiding centre in the international labour movement and that they mean the "enrichment of the Marxist-Leninist theory," as affirmed in the Declaration. The daily practice and life itself will reveal how unreal are the plans that such consultations can "reveal the specific character of the contemporary stage in the development of the society and outline the basic features of the strategy and tactics of communist and workers' parties which correspond to the new conditions," as stated by Suslov in his report submitted at the plenary meeting of the Central Committee of the Communist Party of the Soviet Union. The idea that these consultations may assume the role of an international forum whose decisions are binding for all, that is to play the role of a guiding centre which would replace the previous role of the Executive Committee of the Communist International, is primarily a reflection of an unscientific and subjective approach to the problems of the contemporary social trends in the world, the insufficient viewing of the substance of the problem of the contemporary struggle for socialism and the unsettled problem of what should be the nature of the relations between communist parties, primarily of those communist parties which are in power and whose responsibility as to the future success of the struggle for socialism is by far the greatest. . . .

The Moscow Conference took the line of discovering compromises between different standpoints and tendencies, . . . so that in this statement the standpoints and attitudes which reflected objective contemporary social trends in the world were confronted with bureaucratic-dogmatic concepts, whose most obvious example represents the attitude towards socialist Yugoslavia.

Consequently, there was a possibility of giving most varied interpretations of individual standpoints in the statement, and everything was made in the name of

Marxism-Leninism. The two months since the announcement of this Declaration provide sufficient proof that various parties indicate those viewpoints from this document which are the closest to their own standpoints, while the compromise nature of the statement gives wide possibilities for such interpretations. In that connection there is a very characteristic fact that each communist party would like to prove the correctness of its policy, the continuity of that policy, by underlining that there is no need for any change whatsoever, insisting on the fact that the Conference as such reaffirmed the correctness of its line and practice. Actually, everybody does what he did prior to the publication of this Declaration. Those parties whose policy produce the worst results and which should more thoroughly analyse the causes of the failure in their former activity went to the extreme in this connection.

In the Chinese interpretation of this Declaration the emphasis was placed on the fact that the Communist Party of China had long ago formulated a series of attitudes which are interpreted as new. According to the interpretation published in the Chinese press, it comes out that the 20th Congress of the CPSU did not play a positive role in the consideration of the new political line of the international communist movement, but that this line was outlined as early as ten years ago by Mao Tsetung. As regards the leaders of the Chinese Communist Party, it is very characteristic that they would like to underline their priority, some sort of their monopoly as to the interpretations of contemporary phenomena and developments. In that connection, for instance, it is characteristic that "Jen Min Jih Pao" wrote at the end of the Moscow Conference on November 21, about Mao Tsetung as the only infallible adherent of Leninism in the field of the development of scientific socialism. A series of articles published in China, especially last year, testified to the pretensions of some Chinese leaders to a monopolistic position as regards the interpretation and further development of Marxism. That is why it is not just incidental that those leaders have been striving for priority as regards the interpretation of revisionism, the so-called Yugoslav revisionism in particular. They realize that the entire development of the labour movement is aimed against the monopolistic position of one personality, or of one party, that is, to put it more accurately, of one country. Bringing the so-called struggle against revisionism to an absurd position, they in fact would like to eliminate every opposition to their standpoints and to impose themselves as arbiters of the international communist movement. Obviously, the ultimate product does not only amount to "ideological" monopoly but assumes concrete political forms, being manifested as a tendency to subordinate the principle of the equality of nations to that of "the guiding role."

The future development of events will no doubt again show that arbiters cannot be imposed upon the labour movement as the only authorized interpreters of Marxism, just as no forms of hegemony can be forced upon it. In an equal cooperation between nations on their road to socialism practice as such was and remains the only real judge of the correctness or wrongness of individual attitudes and theories. . . .

THE TREATMENT OF THE REALITY OF SOCIALIST YUGOSLAVIA

In the campaign against socialist Yugoslavia most prominent are the leaders of the Communist Party of China and of the Albanian Workers' Party.

Incidentally I should mention that only one member of the top leadership of the Communist Party of China has visited Yugoslavia, and that at the head of a parliamentary delegation, while not one leader of the Albanian Workers' Party has visited our country since 1948. . . .

It is necessary to point out that from time to time statements are made in certain socialist countries of the desirability of the further development of mutual relations. Even the Soviet Minister of Foreign Affairs, Gromyko, in his report on Soviet foreign policy to the Supreme Soviet, said that "relations with Yugoslavia can be described as good" and he added that one can observe with satisfaction that the attitudes of the two countries coincide on the basic international questions. Gromyko also emphasized that the . . .

"Soviet Government hopes that cooperation between the two countries on the question of the struggle for peace and for relaxation of international tension should continue to develop successfully."

Such statements are certainly positive and should contribute to the creation of a better atmosphere, were they not to conflict with other statements, in which it is asserted that our foreign policy "inflicts damage on the unity of all peace-loving forces and states." It is impossible to reconcile the assertion that the attitudes of the two countries coincide on the basic international questions with an appeal for a struggle against our foreign policy. It is impossible to express the hope for the further development of cooperation between two countries in the struggle for peace and the relaxation of international tension and to attack the peaceful policy of our country.

We know that there are some interpretations which would have it that this is a policy on two separate lines. One, the so-called ideological line, and the other, the line of inter-state relations. It is obvious that these two lines go in two opposite directions. In the relations between socialist countries there cannot exist two lines. Our foreign policy is, for example, both as regards LCY policy and Government policy orientated in the same direction, in the direction of the struggle for peace and the development of all-round relations with all states which wish to cooperate with Yugoslavia on the basis of equality of mutual respect and of non-interference in internal affairs.

Such attitudes towards socialist Yugoslavia create confusion throughout the world, while among us the question arises what sort of policy will be adopted towards our country in the future? Public declarations tend towards a negative policy, with extremely bad consequences, while some official speeches hold out a different prospect. There remains nothing for us to do but express the hope that the interests of the struggle for peace and the strengthening of international cooperation will carry the greater weight in international relations. . . .

ABOUT THE METHOD OF SO-CALLED
IDEOLOGICAL CRITICISMS

It is not at all a secret that the latest Moscow Conference was convened in connection with the dispute about certain stands of the Chinese Communist Party.

However, not a single word is said about this in the Declaration or in subsequent articles and reports at individual plenums. Obviously on account of the fact that it is a question of a great country. Since Yugoslavia is a small country, other rules are applied for her. All means may be used against a small country while unprincipled compromises are made with large countries. What about the observance of the principle of equality in relations between large and small countries? Eventually, what about the principles of Marxism and Leninism to which the Declaration refers so lavishly? The socialist development in individual countries cannot be gauged by the size of the country or by the number of inhabitants. Small socialist countries may also have a more progressive social and economic development, in the socialist sense, than greater or great countries, the same as they may be more backward. Such an attitude towards socialist Yugoslavia proves the political conservativism of the authors of the Declaration in the outlook on and conception of contemporary events in the world, as well as unprincipled opportunism. . . .

ABOUT YUGOSLAVIA'S POLICY OF NON-ALIGNMENT

In the Declaration issued after the Conference of representatives of communist and workers' parties, we find the culmination in the charges against Yugoslavia in the assertion that . . .

"under the pretext of conducting a policy of non-alignment, they (that is, the Yugoslav revisionists) are developing an activity which is inflicting harm upon the unity of all the peace-loving forces and states."

Now one is simply forced to ask: For whom is this slander written? Certainly not for our citizens. And it is not written for the uncommitted countries either because during the long years of their cooperation with us they became acquainted with the basis of our foreign policy, with our firmness and principledness in connection with all more important international problems. And certainly it is not written for the fighters in Algeria who are acquainted with our position in connection with the struggle for liberation, and it is not only since yesterday that they are acquainted with it. And it is not written for the public in the socialist-bloc countries, because that public, despite the campaign and misinformation, that public nevertheless knows, at least roughly, the essence of our policy. For whom is it written, then? Maybe for certain Chinese and Albanian leaders. We leave it to the authors of the Declaration to give the reply. . . .

This attitude towards Yugoslavia unavoidably leads one to the conclusion that the authors of the Declaration in dealing with the problem of war and peace are proceeding from the viewpoint of inevitability of further deepening of the division of the world between the blocs, further grouping of forces around the blocs, and further sharpening of antagonism between the blocs. It is only on the basis of such a logic that it is possible to make attacks on a socialist country, since that country does not belong to either bloc, and the interests of the struggle between the blocs, as some consider, demand the acceptance of the mechanism of the bloc. But this has nothing to do with the proclamation of peace and peaceful coexistence. We do not interpret peaceful coexistence as being a state of existence without a war, under a continuous fear of a war, but rather as an active struggle on the part of all the peace-loving forces for the creation of such relations in which the imperialistic forces, the forces of war, would be completely bridled. Such attacks on the peaceful policy of our country certainly do not serve the interests of rallying together of all the peace-loving forces, but can only cause distrust and suspicion.

In the way in which the policy of co-existence is being treated, one can find a number of other problems as well. One of them is that one does not see in the document who is the partner with whom it is necessary to establish co-existence. Co-existence, as they assert, does not pose a problem between the countries with socialist social systems. The problem of establishment of co-existence with the uncommitted countries which are fighting against imperialism and colonialism, also presents no difficulties. So, there remain only the capitalist countries, primarily those which are grouped around the Atlantic Pact, which possess nuclear weapons. Meanwhile, those countries are not being mentioned as a factor with which it is necessary to conduct negotiations and seek roads which will lead the world from the present-day impasse.

True, in some of the speeches delivered after the Conference in Moscow a greater attention has been paid to the problem of co-existence and fuller interpretations have been given. This is especially reflected into the speech delivered by Khrushchev in the Kremlin on January 6. In that speech the peace-loving policy of the Soviet Union is very strongly stressed, as well as the need of a still more active struggle for peace and for disarmament, for affirmation of the principle of peaceful co-existence. Such an orientation promises that, in the further development of the struggle of the labour movement for peace, against imperialism and colonialism, there will be seen more clearly also the essence of the policy of co-existence in the contemporary conditions. Meanwhile, that is still only a prospect, because one should not forget that not only in the heads of the bourgeois politicians, but also in some of the leaderships of the communist parties, the opinion prevails that co-existence and cold war are a part of a more lasting situation, in the first place in the relations between the blocs, and also in the entirety of international relations. This is illustrated also by the fact that in the Moscow Declaration, and in its subsequent interpretation, there is being stressed the need of affirmation of the principles of co-existence, on the one hand, and on the other hand there is being, in fact, carried out a cold war against the socialist country of Yugoslavia. . . .

Part VII

The 22nd Congress of the C.P.S.U. and the Albanian Issue

The Draft Program of the C.P.S.U., widely circulated in the Summer of 1961, contained no indication that Khrushchev would use the platform of the Soviet Party Congress to raise the Albanian issue.

Although Albania headed the alphabetical listing of states described in the Soviet party draft as members of good standing in the Socialist Camp, she, like Yugoslavia, was not invited to attend the Congress. If Hoxha can be believed, the genesis of the dispute can be traced to a fundamental Albanian disagreement with a whole range of Soviet policies, closely identified with Khrushchev's rise to power. Thus, Khrushchev's advocacy of peaceful coexistence, of the parliamentary road to Socialism, of restraint toward Revisionism, and of the anti-Stalin cult found no favor with the Albanian leadership.

However, more than an argument about policies is involved here. As Albania tells the story, Khrushchev attempted unsuccessfully to use the Bucharest meeting of June 1960 and the Moscow Conference of November 1960 to discipline Albania into ideological compliance. The use now made of a national Party Congress to accomplish the same purpose not only alienated the intended victim, but produced a champion for their cause in the Chinese representative Chou-en-Lai.

Yugoslavia, it may be assumed with a certain satisfaction, chronicled carefully the evidences of obvious strain between the Chinese spokesman and Khrushchev. It was duly noted in the Yugoslav press that Chou-en-Lai did not applaud the Soviet leader's intial speech to the conference and that Chou laid a wreath on Stalin's grave. Whatever significance ought to be attached to such ges-

tures, the Chinese Prime Minister's speech to the Conference indicated, that in addition to old differences about Communist international policy, Chinese-Soviet relations would have to suffer new strains as the result of the mismanagement of intra-camp relations by Khrushchev.

— 22 —

TEXT OF C.P.S.U. DRAFT PROGRAM
1961*

. . . As a result of the devoted labor of the Soviet people and the theoretical and practical activities of the Communist Party of the Soviet Union, there exists in the world a Socialist society that is a reality and a science of Socialist construction that has been tested in practice. The high road to Socialism has been paved. Many peoples are already marching along it, and it will be taken sooner or later by all peoples.

. . . The peoples of Albania, Bulgaria, China, Czechoslovakia, the Democratic Republic of Vietnam, the German Democratic Republic, Hungary, the Korean People's Democratic Republic, Poland and Rumania, and still earlier the people of the Mongolian People's Republic, adopted the path of Socialist construction and, together with the Soviet Union, formed the Socialist camp. Yugoslavia likewise took the Socialist path. But the Yugoslav leaders by their revisionist policy contraposed Yugoslavia to the Socialist camp and the international Communist movement, thus threatening the loss of the revolutionary gains of the Yugoslav people. . . .

The world Socialist system is a new type of economic and political relationship between countries. The Socialist economic basis—social ownership of means of production; the same type of political system—rule of the people

* This selection is excerpted from the text of the draft program of the Soviet Communist Party, which was presented to its Twenty-second Congress in October, 1961. New York *Times,* August 1, 1961. Reprinted by permission.

with the working class at their head; a common ideology —Marxism-Leninism; common interests in the defense of their revolutionary gains and national independence from encroachments by the imperialist camp; and a great common goal—communism. This socio-economic and political community of purpose is the objective ground-work for lasting and friendly intergovernmental relations within the Socialist camp. The distinctive features of the relations existing between the countries of the Socialist community are complete equality, respect for inde-pendence and sovereignty and fraternal mutual assistance. In the Socialist camp or, which is the same thing, in the world community of Socialist countries, none have, nor can have any special rights or privileges.

The experience of the world Socialist system has con-firmed the need for the closest unity of countries that fall away from capitalism, for their united effort in the building of socialism and communism. The line of So-cialist construction in isolation, detached from the world community of Socialist countries, is theoretically un-tenable because it conflicts with the objective laws gov-erning the development of Socialist society. It is harmful economically because it causes waste of social labor, re-tards the rates of growth of production and makes the country dependent upon the capitalist world. It is reac-tionary and politically dangerous because it does not unite, but divides the peoples in face of the united front of imperialist forces, because it nourishes bourgeois-na-tionalist tendencies and may ultimately lead to the loss of the Socialist gains.

As they combine their effort in the building of a new society, the socialist states give active support to and ex-tend their political, economic and cultural cooperation with countries that have cast off colonial rule. They main-tain—and are prepared to maintain—broad mutually advantageous trade relations and cultural contacts with the capitalist countries.

The development of the world Socialist system and of the world capitalist system is governed by diametrically opposed laws. The world capitalist system emerged and developed in fierce struggle between the countries com-posing it, through the subjection and exploitation of the weaker countries by the strong, through the enslavement of hundreds of millions of people and the reduction of entire continents to the status of colonial appendages of the imperialist metropolitan countries. The formation and development of the world Socialist system, on the other hand, proceeds on the basis of sovereignty and free will and in conformity with the fundamental interests of the working people of all the countries of that system.

Whereas the world capitalist system is governed by the law of uneven economic and political development that leads to conflicts between countries, the world Socialist system is governed by opposite laws, which ensure the rapid, steady and balanced growth of the economies of all the countries belonging to that system. Growth of production in a country belonging to the capitalist world deepens the contradiction between countries and intensifies competitive rivalries. The development of each Socialist country, on the other hand, promotes the general progress and consolidation of the world Socialist system as a whole. The economy of world capitalism develops at a slow rate, and goes through crises and upheavals. Typical of the economy of world socialism, on the other hand, are high and stable rates of growth and the common unintermittent economic progress of all Socialist countries.

All the Socialist countries make their contribution to the building and development of the world Socialist system and the consolidation of its might. The existence of the Soviet Union greatly facilitates and accelerates the building of socialism in the people's democracies. The Marxist-Leninist parties and the peoples of the Socialist countries proceed from the fact that the successes of the world Socialist system as a whole depend on the contribution and effort made by each country, and therefore consider the greatest possible development of the productive forces of their country an internationalist duty.

The cooperation of the Socialist countries enables each country to use its resources and develop its productive forces to the full and in the most rational manner. A new type of international division of labor is taking shape in the process of the economic, scientific and technical cooperation of the Socialist countries, the coordination of their economic plans, the specialization and combination of production.

The establishment of the Union of Soviet Socialist

Republics and, later, of the world Socialist system is the commencement of the historical process of an all-round association of peoples. With the disappearance of class antagonisms in the fraternal family of socialist countries, national antagonisms also disappear. The rapid cultural progress of the peoples of the Socialist community is attended by a progressive mutual enrichment of the national cultures, and an active moulding of the internationalist features typical of man in Socialist society.

The experience of the peoples of the world Socialist community has confirmed that their fraternal unity and cooperation conform to the supreme national interests of each country. The strengthening of the unity of the world Socialist system on the basis of proletarian internationalism is an imperative condition for the further progress of all its member countries.

The world Socialist system has to cope with certain difficulties, deriving chiefly from the fact that most of the countries in that system had a medium or even low level of economic development in the past, and also from the fact that world reaction is doing its utmost to impede the building of socialism.

The experience of the Soviet Union and the people's democracies has confirmed the accuracy of Lenin's thesis that the class struggle does not disappear in the period of the building of socialism. The general development of the class struggle within the Socialist countries in conditions of successful Socialist construction leads to consolidation of the position of the Socialist forces and weakens the resistance of the remnants of the hostile classes. But this development does not follow a straight line. Changes in the domestic or external situation may cause the class struggle to intensify in specific periods. This calls for constant vigilance in order to frustrate in good time the designs of hostile forces within and without, who persist in their attempts to undermine the people's power and sow strife in the fraternal community of Socialist countries.

Nationalism is the chief political and ideological weapon used by international reaction and the remnants of the domestic reactionary forces against the unity of the Socialist countries. Nationalist sentiments and national narrow-mindedness do not disappear automatically with the establishment of the Socialist system. Nationalist prejudice and survivals of former national strife are a province in which resistance to social progress may be most protracted and stubborn, bitter and insidious.

The Communists consider it their prime duty to educate working people in a spirit of internationalism, Socialist patriotism and intolerance of all possible manifestations of nationalism and chauvinism. Nationalism is harmful to the common interests of the Socialist community and, above all, the people of the country where it obtains, since isolation from the Socialist camp holds up that country's development, deprives it of the advantages deriving from the world Socialist system and encourages the imperialist powers to make the most of the nationalist tendencies for their own ends. Nationalism can gain the upper hand only where it is not consistently combated.

The Marxist-Leninist internationalist policy and determined efforts to wipe out the survivals of bourgeois nationalism and chauvinism are an important condition for the further consolidation of the Socialist community. Yet while they oppose nationalism and national egoism, Communists always show utmost consideration for the national feelings of the masses.

The world Socialist system is advancing steadfastly toward decisive victory in its economic competition with capitalism. It will shortly surpass the world capitalist system in aggregate industrial and agricultural production. Its influence on the course of social development in the interests of peace, democracy and socialism is growing more and more.

The magnificent edifice of the new world being built by the heroic labors of the free peoples on vast areas of Europe and Asia is a prototype of new society, of the future of all mankind.

The world situation today is more favorable to the working class movement. The achievements of the U.S.S.R. and the world Socialist system as a whole, the deepening crisis of world capitalism, the growing influence of the Communist parties among the masses, and the ideological breakdown of reformism have brought about a substantial change in the conditions of class struggle that is to the advantage of the working people. Even in those countries where reformism still holds strong positions, appreciable shifts to the Left are taking place in the working-class movement.

In the new historical situation, the working class of many countries can, even before capitalism is overthrown, compel the bourgeoisie to carry out measures that transcend ordinary reforms and are of vital importance to the working class and the progress of its struggle for socialism, as well as to the majority of the nation. By uniting large sections of the working people, the working class can make ruling circles cease preparations for a new world war, renounce the idea of starting local wars, and use the economy for peaceful purposes; it can beat back the offensive of Fascist reaction and bring about the implementation of a national program for peace, independence, democratic rights and a certain improvement of the living standard of the people. . . .

The struggle for democracy is a component of the struggle for socialism. The broader the democratic movement, the higher becomes the level of the political consciousness of the masses and the more clearly they see that only socialism clears for them the way to genuine freedom and well-being. In the course of this struggle, Right-Socialist, reformist illusions are dispelled and a political army of the Socialist revolution is brought into being.

Socialist revolutions, anti-imperialist national-liberation revolutions, people's democratic revolutions, broad peasant movements, popular struggles to overthrow Fascist and other despotic regimes, and general democratic movements against national oppression—all these merge in a single revolutionary process undermining and destroying capitalism.

The proletarian revolution in a country, being part of the world Socialist revolution, is accomplished by the working class of that country and the masses of its people. The revolution is not made to order. It cannot be imposed on the people from without. It results from the profound internal and international contradictions of capitalism. The victorious proletariat cannot impose any "felicity" on another people without thereby undermining its own victory.

Together with the other Marxist-Leninist parties, the

Communist party of the Soviet Union regards it as its internationalist duty to call on the peoples of all countries to rally, muster all their internal forces, take vigorous action, and drawing on the might of the world Socialist system, forestall or firmly repel imperialist interference in the affairs of the people of any country risen in revolt and thereby prevent imperialist export of counter-revolution.

It will be easier to prevent export of counter-revolution if the working people, defending the national sovereignty of their country, work to bring about the abolition of foreign military bases on their territory and to make their country dissociate itself from aggressive military blocs.

Communists have never held that the road to revolution lies necessarily through wars between countries. Socialist revolution is not necessarily connected with war. Although both world wars, which were started by the imperialists, culminated in Socialist revolutions, revolutions are quite feasible without war. The great objectives of the working class can be realized without world war. Today the conditions for this are more favorable than ever.

The working class and its vanguard—the Marxist-Leninist parties—prefer to achieve the transfer of power from the bourgeoisie to the proletariat by peaceful means, without civil war. Realization of this possibility would meet the interests of the working class and the people as a whole, it would accord with the national interests of the country.

The working class, supported by the majority of the people and firmly repelling opportunist elements incapable of renouncing the policy of compromise with the capitalists and landlords, can defeat the reactionary, anti-popular forces, win a solid majority in parliament, transform it from a tool serving the class interests of the bourgeoisie into an instrument serving the working people, launch a broad mass struggle outside Parliament, smash the resistance of the reactionary forces and provide the necessary conditions for a peaceful Socialist revolution. This can be done only by extending and continuously developing the class struggle of the workers and peasants and the middle strata of the urban population against big monopoly capital and reaction, for far-reaching social reforms, for peace and socialism.

Where the exploiting classes resort to violence against the people, the possibility of a non-peaceful transition to socialism should be borne in mind. Leninism maintains, and historical experience confirms, that the ruling classes do not yield power of their own free will. Hence, the degree of bitterness of the class struggle and the forms it takes will depend not so much on the proletariat as on the strength of the reactionary groups' resistance to the will of the overwhelming majority of the people, and on the use of force by these groups at a particular stage of the struggle for socialism. In each particular country the actual applicability of one method of transition to socialism or the other depends on concrete historical conditions. . . .

While the principal law-governed processes of the Socialist revolution are common to all countries, the diversity of the national peculiarities and traditions that have arisen in the course of history creates specific conditions for the revolutionary process and for the variety of forms and rates of the proletariat's advent to power. This predetermines the possibility and necessity, in a number of countries, of transition stages in the struggle for the dictatorship of the proletariat, and a variety of forms of political organization of the society building socialism. But whatever the form in which the transition from capitalism to socialism is effected, that transition can come about only through revolution. However varied the forms of a new, people's state power in the period of Socialist construction their essence will be the same—dictatorship of the proletariat, which represents genuine democracy, democracy for the working people. . . .

The Communist movement grows and becomes steeled as it fights against various opportunist trends. Revisionism, Right opportunism, which is a reflection of bourgeois influence, is the chief danger within the Communist movement today. The revisionists, who mask their renunciation of Marxism with talk about the necessity of taking account of the latest developments in society and the class struggle, in effect play the role of peddlers of bourgeois-reformist ideology within the Communist movement. They seek to rob Marxism-Leninism of its revolutionary spirit, to undermine the faith which the working class and all working people have in the Socialist cause, to disarm and disorganize them in their struggle against imperialism. The revisionists deny the historical necessity of the Socialist revolution and of the dictatorship of the proletariat, deny the leading role of the Marxist-Leninist party, undermine the foundations of proletarian internationalism, and drift to nationalism. The ideology of revisionism is most fully embodied in the program of the League of Communists of Yugoslavia.

Another danger is dogmatism and sectarianism, which cannot be reconciled with a creative development of revolutionary theory, which lead to the dissociation and isolation of Communists from the masses of the working people, doom them to passive expectation or incite them to Leftist adventurist actions in the revolutionary struggle, and hinder a correct appraisal of the changing situation and the use of new opportunities for the benefit of the working class and all democratic forces. Dogmatism and sectarianism, unless steadfastly combated, can also become the chief danger at a particular stage of the development of individual parties.

The Communist party of the Soviet Union holds that an uncompromising struggle against revisionism, dogmatism and sectarianism, against all departures from Leninism, is a necessary condition for the further strengthening of the unity of the world Communist movement and for the consolidation of the Socialist camp.

The Communist parties are independent and they shape their policies with due regard to the specific conditions prevailing in their own countries. They base relations between themselves on equality and the principles of proletarian internationalism. They coordinate their actions, consciously and of their own free will, as components of a single international army of labor. The Communist Party of the Soviet Union, like the other Communist parties, regards it as its internationalist duty to abide by the appraisals and conclusions which the fraternal parties have reached jointly concerning their common tasks in the struggle against imperialism, for peace, de-

mocracy and socialism, and by the declaration and the
statement adopted by the Communist parties at their international meetings.

Vigorous defense of the unity of the world Communist
movement in line with the principles of Marxism-Leninism and proletarian internationalism, and the prevention of any action likely to disrupt that unity are an essential condition for victory in the struggle for national
independence, democracy and peace, for the successful
accomplishment of the tasks of the socialist revolution,
for the construction of socialism and communism.

The C.P.S.U. will continue to strengthen the unity and
cohesion of the ranks of the great army of Communists
of all countries. . . .

For the first time in history, a situation has arisen in
which not only the big states, but also the small ones,
the countries which have chosen independent development, and all the states which want peace, are in a position, irrespective of their strength, to pursue an independent foreign policy.

The issue of war and peace is the principal issue of
today. Imperialism is the only source of war danger. The
imperialist camp is making preparations for the worst
crime against mankind—a world thermonuclear war that
can bring unprecedented destruction to entire countries
and wipe out entire nations. The problem of war and
peace has become a life-and-death problem for hundreds
of millions of people.

The peoples must concentrate their efforts on curbing
the imperialists in good time and preventing them from
making use of lethal weapons. The important thing is to
ward off a thermonuclear war, not to let it break out.
This can be done by the present generation.

The consolidation of the Soviet state and the formation of the world Socialist system were historic steps towards the realization of mankind's age-old dream of
banishing wars from the life of society. In the Socialist
part of the world there are no classes or social groups interested in starting a war. Socialism, outstripping capitalism in a number of important branches of science and
technology, has supplied the peace-loving peoples with
powerful material means of curbing imperialist aggression.

Capitalism established its rule with fire and sword, but socialism does not require war to spread its ideals. Its weapon is its superiority over the old system in social organization, political system, economy, the improvement of the standard of living and spiritual culture.

The Socialist system is a natural center of attraction for the peace-loving forces of the globe. The principles of its foreign policy are gaining ever greater international recognition and support. A vast peace zone has taken shape on earth. In addition to the Socialist countries, it includes a large group of non-Socialist countries that for various reasons are not interested in starting a war. The emergence of those countries in the arena of world politics has substantially altered the balance of forces in favor of peace.

There is a growing number of countries that adhere to a policy of neutrality and strive to safeguard themselves against the hazards of participation in military blocs.

In the new historical epoch the masses have a far greater opportunity of actively influencing the settlement of international issues. The peoples are taking the solution of the problem of war and peace into their own hands more and more vigorously. The anti-war movement of the masses, which takes various forms, is a major factor in the struggle for peace. The international working class, the most uncompromising and most consistent fighter against imperialist war, is the great organizing force in this struggle of the people as a whole.

It is possible to avert a world war by the combined efforts of the mighty Socialist camp, the peace-loving non-Socialist countries, the international working class and all the forces championing peace. The growing superiority of the Socialist forces over the forces of imperialism, of the forces of peace over those of war, will make it actually possible to banish world war from the life of society even before the complete victory of socialism on earth, with capitalism surviving in a part of the world. The victory of socialism throughout the world will do away completely with the social and national causes of all wars. To abolish war and establish everlasting peace on earth is a historical mission of communism. . . .

War cannot and must not serve as a means of settling

international disputes. Peaceful coexistence or disastrous war—such is the alternative offered by history. Should the imperialist aggressors nevertheless venture to start a new world war, the peoples will no longer tolerate a system which drags them into devasting wars. They will sweep imperialism away and bury it.

Peaceful coexistence implies renunciation of war as a means of settling international disputes, and their solution by negotiation; equality, mutual understanding and trust between countries; consideration of mutual interests; noninterference in internal affairs; recognition of the right of every people to solve all the problems of their country by themselves; strict respect for the sovereignty and territorial integrity of all countries; promotion of economic and cultural cooperation on the basis of complete equality and mutual benefit.

Peaceful coexistence serves as a basis for the peaceful competition between socialism and capitalism on an international scale and constitutes a specific form of class struggle between them. As they consistently pursue the policy of peaceful coexistence, the Socialist countries are steadily strengthening the positions of the world Socialist system in its competition with capitalism. Peaceful coexistence affords more favorable opportunities for the struggle of the working class in the capitalist countries and facilitates the struggle of the peoples of the colonial and dependent countries for their liberation. . . .

The C.P.S.U. regards Communist construction in the Soviet Union as a component of the building of Communist society by the peoples of the entire world Socialist system.

The fact that Socialist revolutions took place at different times and that the economic and cultural levels of the countries concerned are dissimilar, predetermines the non-simultaneous completion of Socialist construction in those countries and their non-simultaneous entry into the period of the full-scale construction of communism. Nevertheless, the fact that the Socialist countries are developing as members of a single world Socialist system and utilizing the objective laws and advantages of this system enables them to reduce the time necessary for the construction of socialism and offers them the prospect of effecting the transition to communism more or less simultaneously, within one and the same historical epoch.

The first country to advance to communism facilitates and accelerates the advance of the entire world Socialist system to communism. In building communism, the peoples of the Soviet Union are breaking new roads for mankind, testing their correctness by their own experience, bringing out difficulties, finding ways and means of overcoming them, and selecting the best forms and methods of Communist construction.

Since the social forces—the working class, the cooperative peasantry and the people's intelligentsia—and the social forms of economy (enterprises based on the two forms of Socialist property) in the Soviet Union and in the other Socialist countries are of one type, there will be common basic objective laws for Communist construction in the U.S.S.R. and in those countries, with due allowance made for the historical and national peculiarities of each country.

The construction of communism in the U.S.S.R. promotes the interests of every country of the Socialist community, for it increases the economic might and defense potential of the world Socialist camp and provides progressively favorable opportunities for the U.S.S.R. to expand its economic and cultural cooperation with the other Socialist countries and render them assistance and support.

A YUGOSLAV ANALYSIS OF THE DRAFT PROGRAM OF THE C.P.S.U.

September, 1961*

ON THE SO-CALLED LINE OF SOCIALIST CONSTRUCTION IN ISOLATION

The draft program's charges against Yugoslavia focus on the thesis that "the line of socialist construction in isolation" is untenable. The other charges serve chiefly as "deeper" arguments for the main charge. This charge has two purposes: (1) to deny the independent force of Socialist Yugoslavia and (2) to prove that Yugoslavia is trying to isolate herself politically.

First of all, the Yugoslav Communists do not agree that they have taken a line of socialist construction in isolation. On the contrary, they believe Yugoslavia to be objectively and independently—regardless of anybody's desire—a part of the socialist world, and that the Yugoslav Communists are a part of those socialist forces which consistently struggle for new relations between men and peoples throughout the world. History and fact confirm that it is precisely the Yugoslav Communists who have very stubbornly and very consistently fought against the all-too-frequent and very brutal attempts to isolate Yugoslavia in the recent past. For the rest, it is well known who imposed the economic blockade on Yugoslavia and how it was done, who broke economic treaties and other agreements with Yugoslavia and how it was done, and who attempted, and in what way, to isolate the Yugoslav Communists as well as the Yugoslav peoples.

Let us turn, by the way, to the theoretical aspect of this problem. . . .

The thesis that the line of socialist construction in iso-

* *East Europe,* November, 1961. Reprinted by permission.

lation is theoretically untenable, cannot withstand the most superficial scientific criticism. The example of the Soviet Union itself demonstrates that. The construction of socialism is possible even if a country is completely surrounded by capitalism. The example of Yugoslavia refutes this statement only too eloquently; it has succeeded in building socialism, and in strengthening its socialist achievements, despite attempts to isolate it and despite the enormous difficulties imposed by other socialist countries which ought to have been assisting the development of a socialist country.

. . . Since it is not explicitly stated that Yugoslavia is not a socialist country, what then is the purpose of the thesis that the so-called isolated construction of socialism "could ultimately result" in the loss of the socialist accomplishments of the Yugoslav peoples? Obviously this is a restatement of the old thesis, already advanced in the Cominform resolution (of 1948) that the Yugoslav leaders are taking Yugoslavia on the road to perversion of Socialism, that is a "policy of liquidation," etc., etc. Yugoslav practice gives us sufficiently authoritative answers to this "thesis." However, the question arises; if the thesis that socialism depends upon belonging to the socialist camp were correct, what would appear to be the future development of socialism? According to this thesis, socialism would expand only with the expansion of the socialist camp; in this camp a "revolutionary center" would exist and socialism would expand from it in concentrate circles. This is the logic to which the authors of the draft program consistently adhere. . . .

ON RELATIONS AMONG SOCIALIST COUNTRIES

The draft program maintains that the Communist Parties are independent; that they construct their policy on the basis of concrete conditions in their own countries; that they build their mutual relations on the basis of equality and on the principle of proletarian internationalism; that they voluntarily and consciously coordinate their actions. The Yugoslav Communists have struggled consistently for many years to achieve such relations among the Communist Parties. But these claims have a rhetorical sound, because elsewhere the program insists on the unity of the socialist camp and accuses Yugoslavia of creating disunity against the imperialists because of her independent road to socialism. Let us see, therefore, what these statements mean.

There is no disagreement as to the necessity for unity among the anti-imperialist and socialist forces. There is a difference over the question on what basis and by what methods this unity should be achieved. . . . Everyone will agree with the statement in the draft program: "The victorious proletariat cannot impose benefits of any kind without undermining its own victory." Unfortunately, this well-known concept sounds unconvincing in the draft program because our critics consider the links of the socialist camp as the only real unity, in word and in deed, and Yugoslavia is asked to join the camp as a precondition for cooperation with the other socialist countries.

There is no question but that this reveals a policy that ignores the independence of socialist countries; it reveals a bureaucratic-dogmatic conception of the unity of the socialist countries and movements. According to this conception, unity is obviously impossible without a strong camp, without the administrative binding of the socialist countries and Parties in one center. . . . To be brief: the Yugoslav Communists prefer a real unity of free and equal socialist countries and movements, rather than administrative unity. Moreover, this is the only way to overcome the still-existing tendencies toward monopoly and hegemony.

The draft program, it is true, states: "Nobody in the socialist camp or, which is the same thing, in the community of socialist countries, has or can have any special right or privilege whatever." This is a necessary principle. Why, then, despite this principle, is the practice different? . . .

The roots of this practice may be found on another page. We need only examine the claims of the sixth chapter of the second part of the draft program (Communist Construction in the USSR and Cooperation of the Socialist Countries). It says: "The first country to advance to communism facilitates and accelerates the advance of the entire world socialist system to communism. In building communism, the peoples of the Soviet Union are breaking new roads for mankind, testing their correctness by their own experience, bringing out difficulties, finding ways and means of overcoming them, and selecting the best forms and methods of Communist construction."

There is no doubt that the country which first establishes socialist social relations has a special historical role. However, it is strange to emphasize that a country, because it has been the first to take the way to socialism, must for this reason alone develop the best forms and methods for constructing communism.

. . . The Yugoslav Communists, proceeding from the very clear teachings of Lenin, are of the opinion that every country—the Soviet Union as well—goes its specific way to socialism; that there is thus a Soviet way, i.e., the Soviet experience in constructing socialism, and that there are also the practices of other workers' movements and countries, and hence that there are other useful experiences, which, according to existing conditions, can be used by various countries for socialist construction according to the profit which each movement can derive from them. . . .

— 24 —

EXCERPTS FROM CHOU-EN-LAI'S SPEECH BEFORE THE 22ND CONGRESS
October 19, 1961

China has consistently safeguarded its unity with the Soviet Union and the other socialist countries, and, together with them, has consistently waged an unremitting struggle in defense of world peace and in the cause of human progress. We actively support the struggles of the oppressed nations and peoples for their liberation and we firmly oppose the policies of aggression and war pursued by the imperialist bloc headed by the United States.

We have all along advocated and made tremendous efforts to bring about peaceful coexistence among countries with different social systems on the basis of the five principles. . . .

The 1957 and 1960 Moscow conferences of representatives of Communist and Workers Parties were meetings of great historic significance in the international communist movement. The 1957 declaration and the 1960 statement are programs of common action for all the Communist and Workers Parties. Both these documents point out that the unity of the socialist camp, the unity of the international communist movement, is the guarantee of victory for the struggle of the people throughout the world for world peace, national liberation, democracy, and socialism. It is our internationalist obligation as communists to safeguard this great unity.

The declaration and the statement point out that the unity of the socialist camp, the unity of the international communist movement, is the nucleus of all broader world unity. This unity of ours is cemented by common ideals and by a common cause; it has been strengthened and developed in joint struggles against our common enemy and it is based on Marxism-Leninism and proletarian internationalism.

This unity of ours has stood the test of time; no force can destroy it. Our socialist camp, comprising 12 fraternal countries, is a single entity, from the Korean Democratic People's Republic to the German Democratic Republic, from the Democratic Republic of Vietnam to the Albanian People's Republic. We socialist countries and we communist parties of all countries support and cooperate with each other in a brotherly way, on the basis of independence and full equality. We must unite very well and cherish our unity like the apple of our eye and there should absolutely not be any words or deeds that harm this unity.

We hold that if a dispute or difference unfortunately arises between fraternal parties or fraternal countries, it should be resolved patiently in the spirit of proletarian internationalism and on the principles of equality and unanimity through consultations. Any public, one-sided censure of any fraternal party does not help unity and is not helpful in resolving problems. To lay bare a dispute between fraternal parties or fraternal countries openly in the face of the enemy cannot be regarded as a serious Marxist-Leninist attitude. Such an attitude will only grieve those near and dear to us and gladden our enemies. The CCP sincerely hopes that fraternal parties which have disputes or differences will unite afresh on the basis of Marxism-Leninism and on the basis of mutual respect, independence, and equality. This, in my opinion, is the position which we communists ought to take on this question.

The imperialist bloc headed by the United States is now engaged in aggressive and expansionist activities under the cover of anticommunism. U.S. imperialism and the Yugoslav revisionist clique are trying by every means to sow dissension and to disrupt the unity of progressive forces throughout the world. At such time, the unity and solidarity of the entire socialist camp, the unity and solidarity of the entire international communist movement, is of the utmost importance. Unity is strength; unity will triumph over all. In the face of the unity of the forces of socialism throughout the world, the unity of the oppressed nations and oppressed peoples throughout the world, the unity of the peace-loving peoples and countries throughout the world, the imperialists and their followers will suffer complete defeat in all their wild schemes.

Profound friendship has long existed between the peoples of China and the Soviet Union. In both revolution and construction, the Chinese people have enjoyed support and assistance from the people and the CPSU. For this, we again express our heartfelt gratitude. In the cause of building socialism and communism, of opposing imperialist aggression, and of defending world peace, the people of our two countries, together with the people of other socialist countries, have always helped and cooperated with one another, fighting a common struggle and marching forward shoulder to shoulder. This great unity and friendship of the people of our two countries will flow on eternally like the Yangtze and the Volga. . . .

— 25 —

STATEMENT BY THE CENTRAL COMMITTEE OF THE ALBANIAN WORKERS' PARTY

October 20, 1961

Nikita Khrushchev attacked the Albanian Workers' Party at the 22nd CPSU Congress, before the whole world. The anti-Marxist lies and attacks of Nikita Khrushchev serve only the enemies of communism and the Albanian People's Republic—the various imperialists and the Yugoslav revisionists.

Nikita Khrushchev, disclosing to the enemies the misunderstandings which have long existed between the leadership of the CPSU and the Albanian Workers' Party, brutally violated the 1960 Moscow statement which stresses that misunderstandings which arise between the sisterly parties must be patiently settled in the spirit of proletarian internationalism and on the basis of the principles of equality and consultations.

By attacking the Albanian Workers' Party before the whole world, Nikita Khrushchev effectively began an open attack against the unity of the international communist and workers movement, against the unity of the socialist camp. Nikita Khrushchev is fully responsible for this anti-Marxist act and for all consequences which may follow.

Guided by the interests of the unity of the international communist movement and the socialist camp, the Albanian Workers' Party, since the start of our misunderstandings with the Soviet leadership, very patiently tried to settle them in the correct Marxist-Leninist way—the way stressed by the Moscow statement. Nikita Khrushchev, however, chose the anti-Marxist way of irritating these differences—the way of attacks and lies, the way of pressure and threats, and the way of publicly denouncing our misunderstandings.

The Albanian Workers' Party sympathetically received the statement of Comrade Chou En-lai, head of the delegation of the Communist Party of China at the 22nd CPSU Congress, which pointed out that unilateral criticism and public denouncement of misunderstandings existing between the sisterly parties before our enemies cannot be considered a serious and Marxist-Leninist attitude.

From the rostrum of the 22nd CPSU Congress, however, even after this principled statement by the representative of the Communist Party of China, the most eager attacks and slanders against the Albanian Workers' Party and the Albanian People's Republic are being meted out by certain members of the Soviet leadership and by certain leaders of the communist and workers parties of other countries. Thus, they too are assuming a weighty historic responsibility as the dividers of the unity of the international communist and workers movement.

In these conditions—before the organized anti-Marxist attack by Nikita Khrushchev and those who support it, before the slanders and inventions which aim at discrediting our party, and before the serious danger to the future destiny of the unity of the international communist and workers' movement and the socialist camp—the Albanian Workers' Party cannot remain silent. The Albanian Workers' Party will, by means of facts and documents, make known to the whole international communist and workers movement and all international public opinion the whole truth of relations between the Albanian Workers' Party and the leadership of the CPSU, and on which side the truth lies, and will unmask the anti-Marxist and anti-Albanian activities of Nikita Khrushchev and his group.

The unity of the socialist camp and the international communist and workers' movement is being seriously endangered by the anti-Marxist activities of Nikita Khrushchev and his followers.

In this situation, for the protection of the lofty interests of the people and the fatherland and their socialist victories, and the protection of the purity of Marxism-Leninism and the unity of the ranks of the communist movement and the socialist camp, the Albanian Workers' Party, with a clean conscience, has taken and will take all responsibility for any action which it may take before the Albanian people and before the international communist and workers' movement.

The struggle which is being imposed upon our party and people will be a long and a difficult struggle. But difficulties have never frightened our party and people. Our party and people, trained in the struggle against the slanders, attacks, and numerous and continual plots of the various imperialists and Yugoslav revisionists, will also not bend and fall on their knees before the slanderous attacks, blackmail, and pressure of Nikita Khrushchev or of his followers.

The party and the people, with their customary steel-like unity, will determinedly march forward and will triumph on their just road—the road of the triumph of Marxism-Leninism and the cause of socialism and communism. We will win because we are not alone. With us, and with the great cause of Marxism-Leninism, are the communists and the peoples of the Soviet Union, who are linked with us by an invincible friendship and love, which will always live in our hearts regardless of storm and tempest; the communists and the people of China; all the communists of the world; and the peoples of the other socialist countries. The victorious banner of the party—the invincible banner of Marxism-Leninism—will always wave victorious in new socialist Albania.

26

EXCERPTS FROM KHRUSHCHEV'S SPEECH ABOUT ALBANIAN-SOVIET RELATIONS

Delivered to the 22nd Congress
October 27, 1961

The speeches of the delegates and representatives of the fraternal parties show convincingly that the Central Committee of our party acted correctly when it reported to the congress, openly and from a principled standpoint, on the abnormal situation of Soviet-Albanian relations. . . . The Central Committee of our party, showed (greatest patience) and did its utmost to establish good relations between our parties.

The leaders of the Albanian Workers' Party do not hesitate to use any means to conceal from their people the truth as to what our party and people are doing. Albania is the only socialist country which did not publish the full text of the Draft Program of the CPSU.

If they had published it in full, the Albanian working people would have seen where the truth lies and where the lies are. They would have seen that the entire activity of our party and all its plans answer the vital interests of the people, including the interests of the friendly Albanian people.

Our great party has more than once been a target for bitter and foul attacks by the open and hidden enemies of communism. But we do not recall anyone at any time passing at such breakneck speed from expressions and vows of everlasting friendship to unbridled anti-Soviet calumny, the way the Albanian leaders have done.

It seems that they want in this manner to prepare the ground for winning the right to receive alms from the imperialists. The imperialists are always ready to pay 30 pieces of silver to all those who split the communist

ranks. But the pieces of silver have never brought anyone anything but dishonor and ignominy.

We share the anxiety expressed by our Chinese friends
and appreciate their concern for strengthening unity. If
the Chinese comrades wish to make their efforts toward
normalizing the relations between the Albanian Workers'
Party and the fraternal parties, there is hardly anyone
else who can contribute to the settlement of this task more
than the Communist Party of China. This would be, indeed, in the interests of the Albanian Workers' Party,
and would answer the interests of the entire socialist
family.

It is no longer a secret to anyone that the Albanian
leaders maintain their power by resorting to force and
arbitrariness. Today honest people in Albania are being
subjected to repression only because they have the cour-
age to speak in defense of Soviet-Albanian friendship.
Today, advocates for friendship with the USSR and the
CPSU are considered enemies by the Albanian leaders.

This is why the Albanian leaders are against the Leninist course of the 20th party congress. To end the cult of
the individual would mean for Shehu, Hoxha, and others
to renounce, in effect, the key posts in the party and government. It is understood that they will never do it of
their own free will.

We are confident, however, that the time will come
when the Albanian communists and the Albanian people
will have their say, and then the Albanian leaders will be
called to account for the damage they have caused to their
country, their people, and the cause of building socialism
in Albania.

27

MESSAGE OF THE CENTRAL COMMITTEE OF THE CHINESE COMMUNIST PARTY TO THE ALBANIAN WORKERS' PARTY

November 7, 1961

On the occasion of the 20th anniversary of the founding of the Albanian Workers' Party, in the name of all its members and all the Chinese people, the CCP Central Committee sends your party and all your people warmest brotherly greetings.

The founding of the Albanian Workers' Party marked a decisive turn in the history of the Albanian people. From the time of its creation, the Albanian Workers' Party had led the heroic Albanian people in the war of national liberation and has heroically fought the fascist occupiers and the country's traitors. After the liberation, the Albanian Workers' Party lead the Albanian people on the road to successful implementation of the socialist revolution and the building of socialism, and it has, within an historically short period, greatly changed the face of the country and transformed Albania from a backward agrarian and economically poor country to an agricultural and industrial nation. The economic bases of socialism have been established in towns as well as in villages, and now the Albanian people are confidently striving to realize the decisions of the fourth congress of the Albanian Workers' Party and also to fulfill the third five-year plan.

The Albanian people—guided by the Albanian Workers' Party—stand in the fore of the struggle of the socialist camp against the enemies. With a militant spirit, and holding the pick in one hand and the rifle in the other, they have made an active contribution to preserving the cause of socialism and world peace against the imperialist policy of aggression and war. The resolute, principled, and constant fight of the Albanian Workers' Party against contemporary Yugoslav revisionism has played an important role in keeping the purity of Marxism-Leninism intact.

The 20-year history of the Albanian Workers' Party and its activity, struggle, and great successes fully prove that the Albanian Workers' Party is a militant Marxist-Leninist party forged in the (fire?) of revolutionary battles. The Albanian Workers' Party has its roots deep in the people's masses, with whom it is as close as the jaw to the bone.

We are confident that in the future as well, the Albanian people, under the correct guidance of the Central Committee of the Albanian Workers' Party headed by Comrade Enver Hoxha, their tested leader, will certainly score even greater successes in the building of socialism and will make a new contribution in the struggle to support the development of the cause of world peace, democracy, national liberation, and socialism.

The Chinese Communist Party and the Chinese people always follow attentively the struggle of the sisterly Albanian Workers' Party and the brotherly Albanian people, as well as their achievements. The communists and the people of China cordially admire the Albanian Workers' Party and the Albanian people for their revolutionary heroism. The Chinese and Albanian parties and the two peoples are linked by a deep and militant friendship in the common struggle against imperialism, for preserving world peace and building socialism. We are fully confident that the existing friendship and great unity between our two peoples, based on the principles of Marxism-Leninism and international proletarianism, will be strengthened and further developed.

Long live the glorious Albanian Workers' Party. Long live the indestructible unity between the Chinese and Albanian people. Long live the great unity of the socialist camp. Long live the great unity of the international communist movement. Long live victorious Marxism-Leninism.

28

EXCERPTS FROM TITO'S SPEECH ASSESSING THE 22ND CONGRESS AND THE ALBANIAN ISSUE

November 13, 1961

. . . permit me, comrades, to refer briefly to the 22nd CPSU Congress which concluded recently.

We followed attentively the work of this congress and we read what had to do with us. We saw where we were attacked, but we accepted this calmly. We do not agree with this. But we do not dramatize these attacks because they attack us often, and I do not know when they will cease to do so. It would have been much more prudent if there had been less of it.

But we also saw in the work of the congress a positive course, which has already begun to reflect itself effectively on the further development not only in the USSR but in other socialist countries. I think, therefore, that this congress has and will have a great importance for a further movement in a truly democratic and progressive direction, not only in the USSR but in the world in general. . . .

Unfortunately, there were people at this congress who stood firmly by the old Stalinist policies, such as the Chinese delegation and the delegations of some other Asian parties. I do not want to dwell on whether there is anything between the USSR and China and what it is, but it is clear to me that I could never agree, that none of us could agree with the view that the Chinese attitude is positive. That is to say, that it is necessary for the Stalinist line to be reintroduced not only in the USSR but in other countries marching along the road of socialist development. This line would cause much damage not only in the USSR and other socialist countries, but

much more than that, in the general rapid development
of socialism throughout the world and the development
of socialist theory. Accordingly, we could not agree with
such a policy and such a line.

The other thing we noted was that it was the Chinese
party which assumed an incredibly slanderous and sharp
line against our party and against our country at this
congress. Not only this. As far as the Albanian party is
concerned—whose leaders have consistently attacked the
USSR in a provocative manner since the conflict arose
between them and are still doing so—we see that the Albanian party and Enver Hoxha represent the Chinese
party in this part of Europe and trumpet untruths about
us.

The Sino-Albanian speech which some Enver Hoxha
or what is his name read on the occasion of the 20th
anniversary of the Albanian party was riddled with libels
against our country and loaded with assorted fabrications
about alleged dangers which threatened them from us.
In one word, the content was such that you have to
ponder over it and wonder whether there is anything
behind it and what is being prepared. Some provocation
against our country?

We know that something similar was being done in
Stalin's time when provocations were prepared against
us. I say, therefore, that the Albanian leaders represent
a great danger to peace in this part of the world; that
the Chinese leaders are doing mankind a disservice if in
this part of Europe, through the medium of unscrupulous
leaders like Enver Hoxha, Shehu, and others, they want
to cause trouble and foment a new hotbed of war, to
quarrel over our backs with the leaders of the USSR, to
fight against the progressive course which is being followed there. We consider that part of what they say refers
to us, but that a part is addressed to the comrades in
Moscow, to Khrushchev and others. Nevertheless, we
must be vigilant; we must not allow any country, not
even poor misled Albania, to trouble peace here in the
Balkans and cause conflicts to break out.

DATE DUE